Notes on the Occupation

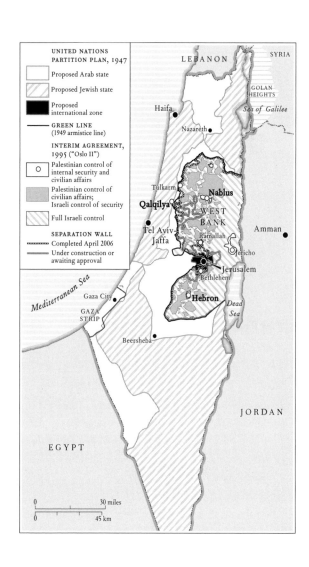

UNITED NATIONS
PARTITION PLAN, 1947

Proposed Arab state

Proposed Jewish state

Proposed
international zone

GREEN LINE
(1949 armistice line)

INTERIM AGREEMENT,
1995 ("Oslo II")

Palestinian control of
internal security and
civilian affairs

Palestinian control of
civilian affairs;
Israeli control of security

Full Israeli control

SEPARATION WALL

Completed April 2006

Under construction or
awaiting approval

LEBANON

SYRIA

GOLAN
HEIGHTS

Sea of Galilee

Haifa

Nazareth

Tulkarm

Nablus

Qalqilya

WEST
BANK

Tel Aviv-
Jaffa

Ramallah

Amman

Jericho

Mediterranean Sea

Jerusalem

Bethlehem

Gaza City

Hebron

Dead
Sea

GAZA
STRIP

Beersheba

JORDAN

EGYPT

0   30 miles

0   45 km

Notes on the Occupation

Palestinian Lives

Eric Hazan

TRANSLATED BY GEORGE HOLOCH

THE NEW PRESS

NEW YORK
LONDON

The New Press gratefully acknowledges the Florence Gould Foundation for supporting the publication of this book.

Originally published in France as *Notes sur l'occupation* by La fabrique éditions, 2006. Published in the United States by The New Press, New York, 2007

Distributed by W. W. Norton & Company, Inc., New York

ISBN 978-1-59558-202-7 (hc)
CIP data available

The New Press was established in 1990 as a not-for-profit alternative to the large, commercial publishing houses currently dominating the book publishing industry. The New Press operates in the public interest rather than for private gain, and is committed to publishing, in innovative ways, works of educational, cultural, and community value that are often deemed insufficiently profitable.

www.thenewpress.com

Composition by Westchester Book Group

Printed in the United States of America

10   9   8   7   6   5   4   3   2   1

CONTENTS

FOREWORD

This is a deceptively simple book. In it Eric Hazan describes what he saw in Palestine under occupation, narrating in the most neutral possible tones the routine, everyday tribulations faced by those he met and spoke with in the West Bank cities of Nablus, Qalqilya, and Hebron. He has cut through the screen of silence, lies, and obfuscation erected around the maltreatment of the Palestinians of the occupied West Bank and Gaza by a Kafkaesque regime of denial of freedom, land theft, and obsessive control of the movement of millions of people. This regime has endured for more than two generations and, far from withering away, is daily becoming more entrenched, more powerful, and more all-encompassing.

In the United States we do not see these simple realities because we are not allowed to see them. We do not see them because so much is invested either in our "seeing" things through the eyes of those who impose or support this occupation, or, more frequently, through the blank eyes of those who refuse to see it or its effects on the occupied (and the occupiers). The very fact that there is an occupation—since 1967, the most important fact in the lives of millions of Palestinians—is itself rarely touched upon in what little we do read, see, and hear of occupied Palestine. This Potemkin village vision is imposed on us via the media and in political discourse, where it is rarely challenged. And when the victim occasionally is allowed to testify, the victimizer is always wheeled in—in the name of "balance"—to get the last word.

Few in number and brave indeed are those who have been willing to confront openly this smug consensus that blandly elides forty years of occupation (and nearly two decades of dispossession before that) and asserts that, in any case, the suffering on both sides is mainly the Palestinians' own fault. The Palestinians have never missed an opportunity to miss an opportunity, we are told, and they are doubly guilty for having obliged otherwise pure Israelis to respond, with the greatest reluctance, to their appalling behavior. Blaming the victims, as Edward Said so memorably put it, is still the standard approach to this entire issue.

Hazan has the courage and vision to cut through such cant. He understands the historical dimension of what he saw in Palestine, and he has a deep and profoundly political understanding of what oppression, colonialism, and occupation mean. When Hazan writes that in the eyes of the oppressors, the only good oppressed is an obedient one; when he says there is no Israeli–Palestinian conflict, only a people that resists the army of occupation and the settlers as best they can; he shows perceptiveness and bravery. He reminds us of earlier colonial wars, when identical tropes were deployed in justification of the continued maintenance of an unequal and unjust order. He sees beyond Palestine to other occupations, to other colonial realities, where the weak were the victims of the strong. He also shows deep wisdom about the universal values at stake in Palestine, and the true moral dimensions of what is going on in that tortured country. And he shows quiet outrage at the silence that envelops these terrible occurrences.

But this is not a polemical book. It is an elegantly conceived and eloquently written piece of reportage by an honest man about the general state of imprisonment imposed on the Palestinians in the West Bank and Gaza Strip. Hazan simply tells us what that is like, in unadorned prose. Any American journalist among the many hundreds who have passed through occupied Palestine over the past forty years could have done this (though whether their employers would have allowed their work to see the light of day is another matter), but only a very few could have equaled the clarity of vision and moral purpose that Hazan brings to this task.

This is a book that should be as widely read as possible, ideally by those who consider the very term occupation to be "controversial," or do not understand—because they have never been allowed to learn—just what this occupation consists of. Fortunately, there is clearly a growing interest in the United States in knowing about the realities of Palestine and Israel, and a thirst for greater understanding that people feel has been denied them.

Perhaps Americans are now more willing to think about these hard issues because of what is now nearly universally acknowledged to be the disastrous results, in Iraq and elsewhere, of the Bush administration's botched Middle East policies. Perhaps they are more focused than before because the Iraq disaster comes after trends originating in the Middle East produced the savage terrorism that struck the United States on 9/11. Perhaps the connection is becoming clearer between the Bush administration's hostility to the Palestinians and its unlimited support for the most extreme Israeli policies, and the widespread unpopularity of the United States in the Middle East. And perhaps there is a new receptivity because of the dangerous new world we all find ourselves in today. Whatever the reason, some people at least have begun to understand that what is being done in Palestine with full American support causes grave and continuing harm to the interests of the United States, its image, and its moral standing.

Hazan's notes about the workings of the great military-bureaucratic machine that controls all aspects of the lives of several million Palestinians are straight-forward. They underline the basic realities of occupation that are understood throughout the Arab and Islamic worlds, and in most of the rest of the world. Only in America do these realities continue to be successfully obscured, elided, and denied. One can only hope that through testimonies like Hazan's, Americans will increasingly come to see these realities as they are, and not as the apologists for occupation prefer that they see them. Perhaps then something will be done to change the longstanding American policies that underwrite the imprisonment and immiseration of the Palestinian people, making a just and lasting peace in Palestine and Israel impossible.

—Rashid Khalidi
Edward Said Professor of Arab Studies
Columbia University Press
New York, February 18, 2007

PREFACE

You know as well as we do that, when these matters are discussed by practical people, the standard of justice depends on the equality of power to compel and that in fact the strong do what they have the power to do and the weak accept what they have to accept.

Thucydides, *The Peloponnesian War*, V.4.89.
(The Athenians to the Melians)

These *Notes on the Occupation* were taken in May and June 2006, a period of calm in the West Bank when a half-dozen young men at most were killed every week. To see the everyday operation of the vast military and bureaucratic machine known as the "occupation," I had selected three cities—Nablus, Qalqilya, and Hebron—based on what I had heard about them: three exemplary cases, but each one with a different history, a different geographical situation, and a different form of imprisonment.

Soon after I returned home, acts of resistance against the army of occupation set the offended Israeli war machine in motion, bringing about the devastation of what remained of the Gaza Strip and then of southern Lebanon, exodus, and hundreds of deaths. Palestine suddenly disappeared from the headlines to be replaced by Israeli Army spokesmen, humanitarian hand-wringing, Condoleezza Rice, and the geopoliticians.

There is one constant, one obsessive theme in the words of the ministers, presidents, and generals of the Holy Alliance: punish, clean up, finish off. Whether the subject is Baghdad, Bobigny, or Rafah, differences of culture and situation cannot succeed in concealing the similarities. In the eyes of the oppressors, a good oppressed is a peaceable, and if possible silent, oppressed. If he rebels, depending on circumstances it will be said that he despises our values, that he is engaging in provocation, that he cultivates gratuitous violence, or that he belongs to a terrorist organization. No matter what, he is wrong.

This is why the Palestinians have such a bad press. In reality, there is no peaceable situation in Palestine: there is the everyday condition of military occupation and collective punishment that the population of the West Bank and Gaza have suffered under for forty years, sometimes patiently, sometimes not. Nor is there an Israeli–Palestinian conflict: there is a people that resists the settlers and the army of occupation as well as it can, despite the complicity of the "Western democracies," all the Arab governments, and some of their own leaders.

The dominant discourse seeks to make the real situation indecipherable. It works to mask the link between the destruction of Gaza, military control of the West Bank settlements, and the invasion of Lebanon. It attempts to use the Sunni–Shiite division to obscure the terrible shared fate of the people of southern Lebanon and the Palestinian people. More than anything, it strives to conceal the fact that the origin of the current devastation in the Middle East is to be found neither in Iran nor in Syria, nor God knows where—that it is contained within the Palestinian pressure cooker whose temperature and tension I have attempted to describe in these *Notes*.

August 2006

ACKNOWLEDGMENTS

Veteran journalist and peace activist Michel Warschawski encouraged me in this project and organized my journey with his usual care. He read the manuscript, as did Eyal Sivan, Sabrina Berkane, Stéphane Passadéos, and Joëlle Marelli: the final text owes a good deal to their criticisms and friendly suggestions.

The real authors of this book are the men and women who welcomed me and guided me in Palestine, who trusted me, and answered my questions. May all the divinities of the region protect them.

I. NABLUS

On the road from Ramallah to Nablus, the checkpoint on the way into the city is deserted at night. Anyone who wants to join the bad guys can. The bad reputation of Nablus is nothing new. In the late 1930s, at the time of the Arab rebellion, the song was already familiar: "Nablus city of soap, Nablus city of cakes, Nablus home of the resistance." Since the media dubbed it a "nest of terrorists" at the beginning of the Second Intifada,[1] the city has been punished by the occupation forces to a degree that has no equivalent in the West Bank, or anywhere else for that matter: with no wall, no barbed wire, no watchtowers, Nablus is encircled.

The city is located at the bottom of a deep valley. At either end, the major roads are blocked by checkpoints, Hawarra on the south, on the road to Ramallah and Jerusalem, and Beit Iba on the northwest road to Qalqilya and Jenin. Of the secondary roads leading to nearby villages, some are controlled by the Israeli army (seven checkpoints distributed around the city), and others are closed off by concrete blocks, metal fences, or, for the narrowest, mounds of earth or trenches.

From the terrace of Y.'s house—he will be my host and guide in Nablus—glimmering through the darkness, on the summits of the two mountains overlooking the city, are the lights and the tall antennas of Israeli military camps. On the slopes between the city's last buildings and the camps, a wide security zone with no houses and no vegetation, illuminated by searchlights, makes it possible to shoot on sight anyone attempting an unauthorized exit in that direction to avoid the checkpoints on the roads.

Anyone under the age of thirty is systematically turned back at the checkpoints. (Right now. At other times, the only ones allowed through are boys under sixteen and married men over fifty.) This means that since the reoccupation of the West Bank in the spring of 2002, many of the 160 thousand inhabitants of Nablus have never left the city.

In the old city (the Casbah), at the bottom of the valley, the devastation of April 2002 is not confined to one area but scattered through a solid urban fabric that even armored bulldozers could not damage as widely as they did the camp in Jenin. The most venerable buildings were the ones that were dynamited. In front of gaps between buildings, I'm told that here was a caravansary, there a traditional soap factory, and over there a house that had been famous for centuries. In places amid the rubble, plaques indicate that international institutions will endeavor to repair the damage. In reality, the destruction goes on every day: In every nighttime "incursion," the vehicles that the inhabitants call jeeps, which are really command cars with reinforced armor, race through lanes and markets shattering everything in their paths. The damage, the traces of bullets, are visible at every step. The walls are covered with pictures of "martyrs" [I do not like that word]. Some posters are almost completely bleached by the sun; others are perhaps only a week old. People here proudly assert that their dead are more numerous than the dead of Jenin and that 20 percent of the ten thousand prisoners held in Israel come from the region.

At 7 A.M. a local radio station broadcasting from An-Najah University presents the local news: weather at the checkpoints, army "incursion" last night in Balata refugee camp—a suburb—or in the old city. The announcer's tone is often mocking. This morning (May 31, 2006): "*Sabah el Kheir* [good day] to all the inhabitants of Nablus. Good day as well to the sellers of gas canisters who are taking advantage of the shortage to increase their prices from 35 to 45 shekels [one shekel is worth a little less than a quarter]. Good day to them and to all the exploiters of the Palestinian people!"

Y. is French, but Nablus is a second home for him. He established Darna (translated "our house"), which has taken in and offers guidance to forty associations in the city and the neighboring refugee camps. One association organizes the teaching of English by volunteers passing through; another helps children in the camps organize exhibitions of drawings; still others work on repairing demolished houses, establishing links between young people in East Jerusalem and the West Bank. In Darna, nothing resembles a nongovernment organization (NGO), no high salaries, 4×4s, official visits, or wannabe adventurers: it is a center of resistance. Y., whose native language is Arabic, travels night and day on foot around a city where almost everyone greets him—a fish in water, as Mao used to say.

★ ★ ★

Outside of periods of intense confrontation, the army of occupation does not enter Nablus in daylight. When a military vehicle ventures in, stones immediately fly. But soldiers make "incursions" every night, sometimes into the old city, a warren hospitable to fugitives, sometimes into one of the two large refugee camps, Balata and Askar. Every night shots can be heard, the boom-boom of Israeli heavy weapons, the rat-tat of Palestinian rifles. Sensible inhabitants don't go out after 11 P.M. because it seems it's not a good idea to come across special forces squads dressed as Palestinians preparing their operations—kidnappings, targeted assassinations. There is a de facto curfew.

Hamas[2] 1. *In Balata.* Southwest of the city, this camp shelters, so to speak, twenty thousand refugees or descendants of refugees of 1948, most of them from the areas of Jaffa, Lydda, and Haifa. I meet S., a Hamas member of the camp committee.

"What relations does the camp have with the society of Nablus?"

"They are good because we have the same difficulties as the people of the city, and we share the same goals." [Next comes a long disquisition on the unity of the resistance, an example of what Amira Hass calls "heroic blabla."]

"I ask this question because I was in Ramallah last

year and I thought I understood that relations between the population of the city and the population of Al Amari camp were not at all good. And here?"

"Yes, there is conflict between the camp and the city. The people of Nablus do not feel at all concerned by the camp; they don't see why they should make room for us, or why they should pay for our water and electricity. Most important, the level of militancy is much higher in the camp than in the city. Many think of us as extremists, dangerous people who make trouble for them."

"Does operation of the camp still depend entirely on the United Nations Relief and Works Agency (UN-RWA[3]) [for Palestinian Refugees in the Near East], or is there aid from the municipality of Nablus or the Palestinian Authority?"

"Until the 1980s, the UNRWA covered all our needs, education, health, etc. They set up the water and sewer systems in the camp. They even served lunch to children in the schools. Their aid significantly decreased at the time of the Lebanon war. Now, for example, health coverage is only partial, and people have to pay a quarter or half of their medical expenses. Food aid is limited to occasional emergency distributions.

"As for the municipality, it supplies water and electricity, and it picks up the garbage we deposit at the entry to the camp."

"To what do you attribute this decrease in aid from the UNRWA?"

"The chief supplier of funds to the UNRWA is the United States. It has greatly reduced its contribution for political reasons, to put pressure on the refugees, to make us more dependent, more vulnerable."

"How does a camp like Balata participate in elections in Palestine?"

"Refugees do not participate in local elections, not in Balata and not in the other camps in Palestine. But we vote and can run in national legislative elections. In the parliament that has just been elected, there are two representatives from the camp (not elected by the camp, but coming from the camp): a woman, a Hamas representative, and a representative elected on Fatah's[4] national list."

"What has happened in the camp in the last few days?"

"During the past week, three young men were killed, and others were wounded or arrested."

"It was an ordinary week?"

"Yes."

We go out for a tour of the camp, which resembles others I know: a neighborhood on the outskirts of the city, more miserable than the miserable streets leading to it. A good deal of damage caused by bulldozers and tanks, traces of bullets on all the buildings.

[walking] *"Has the boycott of the Hamas government had an effect on the standard of living in the camp?"*

(gently) "It's not the Hamas government; it's the elected government of the Palestinian people. On the standard of living, yes, indirectly: in this camp there are at least one thousand employees of the Authority who have not been paid for three months."

"Were you born here?"

"Yes, but it's not my native land. My native land is Jaffa. Before he died, my father gave me the key to his house there."

On one of the summits overlooking Nablus, there is an unexpected monument, a full-sized replica of the Villa Rotonda of Palladio. Contrary to what one might think, this is not the fantasy of some rich nineteenth-century Anglo-Turkish merchant. It was constructed recently by the millionaire heiress of a great Nablus family, the Masris. The idea, a plausible one, was that the place was in danger of being taken over by the army. The heiress gave her villa to Yasir Arafat to serve as a residence for distinguished guests of Palestine.

Hamas 2. I ask H., who works in the French cultural center, if it's because of the Hamas municipal government that there are no movie theaters in Nablus.

"Not at all! It was the Al-Aqsa Brigades[5] that burned down the three theaters in the city."

"But aren't they secularists?"

"No, they're hoodlums. They're the only ones you see carrying weapons in the street. In every neighborhood there is a brigade, made up of dangerous people, not really members of the Al-Aqsa resistance, who are dead or in prison. In the West Bank at least, Hamas doesn't parade through the streets, especially not bearing arms. It has nothing to do with the banning of alcohol and public entertainment. The municipal government doesn't give the cultural center any trouble about concerts and film showings; quite the opposite."

"Hamas got 77 percent of the votes in municipal elections here, thirteen out of fifteen seats on the city council. There is nothing bad to say about the mayor, the owner of the Mercedes franchise in Nablus. A few weeks ago, when a young German in Darna was briefly kidnapped, he came to see the foreigners in the center, all alone, and he said to them: 'Stay with us. If you don't feel safe, come and live in my house.' While this was going on,

Médecins sans frontières and Médecins du monde were packing up and leaving in their big 4×4s."

Before I set out on my trip, Michel Warschawski explained to me that when people speak of the "Hamas landslide," they forget that Palestinian legislative elections are in two parts, one with proportional voting from nationwide lists, and the other by majority vote in local constituencies. In proportional voting, Hamas won by only a slim majority. It won large majorities in local voting: the Palestinians rejected one by one the Fatah candidates. Several of the men and women I met told me they were "leaning toward Fatah," or even "Fatah by conviction," but that they had voted Hamas this time to get rid of a particular Fatah notable, a notoriously corrupt collaborator.

Seen on an election poster in the street: the candidate poses in front of a plane. He is an old Fatah leader who was for a time in charge of the Gaza airport. He conducted his campaign on this theme: I've made a good bit of money, so you might as well vote for me instead of someone new who will put his hands in the till.

Clan Solidarity. When we go out in the morning, we say hello to the superintendent for the block of houses. Y. explains that his wife is taking courses at An-Najah University, at a cost of 500 shekels [about US $125] per term. They have two children. They manage financially only because they have family living abroad, in Jordan and the Gulf, who send them money. Even in refugee camps, clans from villages driven out in 1948 have reconstituted themselves: in Balata there is the "family N" or the "family Z" neighborhood. This is one of the principal reasons why Palestine—and encircled Nablus in particular—has not sunk into poverty. During the election campaign, when Fatah tried to frighten people by telling them: "If you vote for Hamas, you will get no more international aid," they paid no attention, because they'd never seen a drop of it, and they have survived thanks to clan solidarity. A., who occasionally comes to have a whiskey on Y.'s terrace, has made a specialty out of tracking down families abroad on behalf of the poorest. It doesn't matter if they are distant cousins; help for those who have stayed in Palestine is an obligation.

The same thing happens at a higher level. A "wealthy bourgeois" who lives in Y.'s building— impeccable striped shirt, polished black shoes—is a member of a family that built an entire city in Saudi Arabia and owns property in Jordan. He is the only one who stayed in Nablus. The others send him money, so he can keep his furniture factory running, even at 30 percent capacity, and allow thirty workers to support themselves and their families.

We visit two merchants downtown, one who sells local agricultural products (oil, fruit syrups); the other, chocolate. Both work in modern offices, air conditioned and equipped with up-to-date computers. Y. advises them on organizing their exports to go through Jordan instead of Israel. He tells me that they could make twenty times as much elsewhere and live better, but they made the choice of staying in Nablus. They are not political, but they are attached to their city.

A Hero of Our Time. Bassam Shakaa was mayor of Nablus in the 1970s. After the forces of occupation had tried everything to make him bend, a bomb was finally set off in his car. This attack, which made him famous around the world, cost him his two legs. He tells his story.

"I was born into a well-off family, in which no one was interested in farming. I was the only one of all my brothers and sisters who spent time with the workers who cultivated our land. That was how I started to get interested in the cause of Palestine. At the time of the Nakbah in 1948, I was seventeen and in high school. I left school and joined the Palestinian fighters. After the defeat, knowledge of the plot between King Abdullah and the state of Israel[6] and the attitude of the Western countries led me to join the Baath Party, which was at the time the party of Arab unity.

"Between 1954 and 1957, we succeeded in doing away with the Baghdad Pact, which had made Iraq into a veritable colony, and we fought against the alliance between Britain and Jordan. We elected deputies to the Jordanian parliament in 1955,[7] and we pushed the government to strengthen its alliance with Egypt and Syria. But these first steps toward unity were no match for maneuvers by the West and the Israelis. In the late 1950s, King Hussein[8] entered the American orbit and unleashed repression against the democratic parties. Many of us were imprisoned or murdered. I went into hiding, and, from 1957 to 1959, I continued working with party cells here, in the surrounding villages and the city of Nablus.

"In 1959, along with several comrades from the region, I participated in the Baath Party conference in Beirut, and we realized then that some forces in the party were working for a split: there were the pro- and anti-Nasser camps. We thought that Arab unity was important. At the time of the split between the Iraqi and Syrian branches, we left the Baath Party and continued to campaign for unity from the outside. I stayed in Syria with some comrades from 1959 to 1961; we could no longer enter Palestine through Jordan, everything was blocked off, and we were being hunted down. In Syria, we worked constantly to restore party unity, but I was soon put in prison: they came to get me in the hospital where my wife, who was also a party activist, had just given birth. We were expelled from the country, and we ended up as political refugees in Cairo, where I stayed for three years. Then King Hussein declared an amnesty, and I was able to come back here.

"The Jordanians put me in prison again in 1966, along with three of my brothers, after the Israeli attack on the village of Samur. I was known as a militant who supported the autonomy of Palestine, which was prohibited at the time. When the Israelis occupied the West Bank in 1967, I was among the first to set up popular committees for resistance. The Israelis captured me and wanted to deport me to Jordan, but my uncle, who was then the mayor of Nablus, intervened to prevent that. Since 1967, I have constantly campaigned for the unity of Palestine, for the recognition of the Palestine Liberation Organization (PLO) as its representative body, and against what the Israelis proposed, that is, a Palestinian protectorate in the West Bank. What the Oslo Accords meant—a Palestinian government to carry out Israeli policies—is something I have always rejected.

"In 1976, the Israelis accepted the creation of municipal councils in the West Bank to apply their policies. I was rather in favor of boycotting the elections, but I gave in to pressure from my comrades: we participated, and we won the election in Nablus. We won a number of cities in the West Bank and Gaza on lists calling for national unity and the rejection of collaboration. We managed to defeat the Israeli plan for a Palestinian mini-state that would be under their domination. When the Camp David Accords (the peace agreement between Israel and Egypt in 1978) were reached, there was heavy pressure to create that kind of state. We organized the resistance with the parties, unions, and civic groups, and the Israelis were unable to impose their law. We did everything possible to organize an economy here that would not be dependent on Israel, by launching a campaign for the electrification of Nablus and the region, by establishing our own water company. . . .

"There were 1,200 military orders and regulations in the West Bank, and we obeyed none of them. For example, we were forbidden to build schools: we built schools. City government funds were supposed to go through an Israeli bank: we refused, and not a penny went to Israel.

"After this action by the city government, the

Israelis started to put pressure on me by threatening my family. One of my daughters was put in prison. The military governor came to see me and said: 'Why didn't you tell me your daughter had been arrested?' I answered: 'You think she's the only girl in prison? There are dozens of girls in your prisons.' My son was also jailed for three months, after which they said he could pay a fine to be released. He refused, and he stayed in prison. We used to have a soap factory in Nablus: the Israelis prevented oil deliveries, and they froze our accounts in a Jordanian bank. The friends who came to see me were harassed, and so were their families, merely because they came to visit me.

"In 1979, the Israelis arrested me and decided to deport me. A large unified movement sprang up: the leaders of civic groups, sporting clubs, the chamber of commerce, parties, and unions, and the members of the municipal councils threatened mass resignations. The Israelis had to give up the idea of deporting me. They offered to allow me to live quietly if I were to resign as mayor. I told them to ask for the opinion of the city council. The Red Cross was supposed to accompany me when I was deported. I asked them if they weren't ashamed to be accomplices in a war crime—they apologized. Finally, I went on a hunger strike for fourteen days, and the army let me go.

"At the time, the Israeli defense minister, Ezer Weizmann, threatened me with physical reprisals. I asked him why he was doing that. He answered that I had initiated the first demonstration against the establishment of settlements on the West Bank. I asked him who was breaking the law, people establishing illegal settlements on occupied land or people demonstrating against them. But I knew, I had a premonition that I was going to be killed.

"Six months later, they put a bomb in my car. After the explosion, I crawled out and asked a passer-by to call my wife, but the phone lines in the house and in the hospital had been cut. I was picked up by a private car, and that's what saved me. They thought I was going to die; the doctors said it was better to let me go in peace. Finally, they amputated both legs above the knee. When I woke up, I yelled at the doctors who didn't want reporters to come to see me. I gave my first interview when I'd barely come out of the operating room.

"During my convalescence, I spent a week in France with other Palestinian mayors. We were warmly welcomed, and we held a rally at the Mutualité, which was a great success despite attempts by Zionist militants to disrupt it. When I got back to Nablus, a sea of humanity was waiting for me. I was still the mayor, under surveillance every minute of the day by the Israeli services. No one could come to see me without being investigated, even the English consul. The soldiers threatened to remove him from my house by force, and they questioned him outside my door for twenty minutes. He was ashen when he came in.

"This ordeal lasted for years. I had artificial legs at the time, and when I went out, I was surrounded by plainclothes police. Whoever greeted me was hit right in front of me. The Israelis finally dissolved the city council in 1982. The employees went on strike and refused to work under a military governor. Following discussions with Arafat, the municipal government was turned over to the Nablus chamber of commerce in 1986. These were the beginnings of the Oslo negotiations."

"What was the point at which the process that led to the Oslo Accords began?"

"At Camp David in 1978, and with [Anwar Al] Sadat's trip to Jerusalem. That's when we detected the first signs of an agreement between some Palestinian leaders and the Israelis. But they still had to stay hidden, because the executive committee of the PLO was opposed to contacts of that kind. After the invasion of Lebanon in 1982, what it was leading to was clearer: the Palestinians would be given some degree of autonomy in return for applying Israeli policies. When we understood what was brewing, in the late 1980s, we sent a message from the Nablus city council to the executive committee demanding Arafat's resignation.

"Neither the leadership of the PLO, nor even that of Fatah, was aware of the Oslo negotiations. They were secret agreements made behind the backs of the Palestinian and Arab peoples."

"What should have been done at the time?"

"We shouldn't have made concessions; we should have stuck to our guns. We got nothing by giving in, and that was to be expected. The pseudo-peace process accelerated the colonization of the West Bank and intensified repression. Before Oslo, the Israelis were facing a population of resistance fighters; they couldn't get away with everything. Oslo demobilized the people."

"What do you think of the joint action of people in the villages and Israeli activists around the wall?"

"We can't help but salute the actions of those Israelis. I respect them and some of them are my friends. Ten years ago Israeli society was more open than it is now. I think these little groups serve primarily the Israeli media machine, demonstrating that there is complete freedom in the country to express one's opposition. Their form of struggle remains very symbolic and not seriously dangerous for the state. And we also have to recognize that our own lack of media resources makes it hard for us to use these movements for our own cause."

"Why are there never any Palestinian voices directed to the outside world, which is waiting with open ears?"

"The reason is that we have a resistance without a political policy. The Palestinian Authority is opposed to the resistance. Before Oslo, everyone understood our position because resistance and politics went hand in hand. Now we have against us not only Israel and the Americans, not only all the Arab countries, but also some of the Palestinian leadership."

"Do you think the current attitude of Hamas, which rejects negotiations, represents a chance to return to a sounder view of the resistance?"

"I have a friend in Nazareth who is a Christian. I thought he would be shattered by Hamas's victory. Not at all; he was very happy: 'For once we're going to have Palestinians who say no!' The reaction from the West [the boycott of the government] is normal; they realize that the cycle of endless concessions is threatened, that there's a risk the hemorrhage will stop. That's why you see Abu Mazen[9] hand-in-hand with Israel and the Americans, doing everything he can to bring down the Hamas government. In the current internal Palestinian negotiations [between Hamas and Fatah],

I sent a letter to indicate my complete opposition to Abu Mazen's positions. I wrote:

> After more than fifteen years of [Oslo] negotiations, what national rights has our people obtained? The final result was determined by agreement between the occupying power and the sponsor of the negotiations, the United States, in a letter George Bush wrote to Sharon after their April 14, 2004 summit meeting—a letter that our people sees as a new Balfour Declaration. This letter finally put an end to the illusion that a Palestinian state could be established through negotiations. This is why I ask everyone who is participating in this dialogue among Palestinians to reread that document to persuade themselves that negotiations like the Oslo negotiations can lead to nothing, even if some people keep hanging onto them, forgetting that our people has rejected the idea of negotiating, as the results of the legislative elections have demonstrated.

"If you had to define yourself politically, what word would you choose?"

"Citizen."

Morning news (June 3) on Radio Najah: last night, soldiers entered Nablus hospital and took away a wounded man. In response, Palestinians later attacked the military camp on the hill overlooking our building (indeed, sounds of firing had seemed closer than usual).

The United States is threatening banks that agree to transfer foreign funds to the Palestinian government with sanctions. The Arab Bank, which operates as a central bank in Palestine, has blocked the transfer of funds corresponding to the value-added tax to the elected government. It is clear to everyone I speak to that the Fatah presidency, the Americans, and the Israelis are organizing shortages—gasoline yesterday, gas canisters today—to provoke a popular movement against Hamas. *Al-Quds*, the principal Palestinian newspaper, publishes a front-page photograph of a crowd with the caption: "In Gaza, policemen and soldiers demonstrate against poor handling of the crisis by the Hamas government." One thinks of the truck drivers' strike in Chile and all the other Central Intelligence Agency maneuvers leading up to Allende's fall.

A Soap Fanatic, a Book Fanatic. To get to Beit Furik, a little village northeast of Nablus, you go through a rural checkpoint where passage is at the whim of bored soldiers. B. is waiting for us at the door to his small factory. His parents, who owned

a traditional soap factory in town, had forced him
to go to school, but once he'd passed his last exam,
he'd brought them his framed diploma as a present and told them that what interested him was
making soap. After the family business in the old
city was destroyed three times by the army, he decided to set himself up here in Beit Furik. He
makes all the machines, copying Italian and Israeli
models. He is an experimenter, who invents all
kinds of soaps, with lemon, honey, figs. He works
with Israeli cooperatives—Communists, he tells
us, but not only with them. He is the one who
produces a large portion of the soaps made with
mud from the Dead Sea: in the midst of the Intifada, the Ahava (love) Company asked him to
come to Ashdod to do business with them ("They
greeted me like the Messiah!") The tourists who
buy this soap on the shores of the Dead Sea and
elsewhere certainly have no idea where it comes
from, but it's a limited market. To sell what he
produces, B. has to be able to use trucks, and to
have trucks travel, he needs an authorization, a
"special permit to go through internal checkpoints in Judea and Samaria."[10] For that, he has to
secure permissions from the "Coordination" in
Nablus (a term dating from the Oslo Accords
when the Israeli and Palestinian security services
worked more or less together. Now the Israelis

coordinate with themselves). The Coordination sometimes grants permission, often refuses, so that B.'s warehouses are filled with tons of soap that he cannot get out of Palestine. So, he says, laughing, he gives gifts.

Before the Intifada, there were many small factories like B.'s in Nablus, metal and textile factories (most Orthodox Jewish clothing, it seems, was made in Nablus). The encirclement of the city forced them to close or to reduce production to the point where they were no longer profitable.

For twenty years, K. has been running the only Marxist bookstore in Palestine, the People's Bookstore, in the heart of Nablus. He sells the communist classics, books on the resistance, cassettes of revolutionary songs. His bestsellers are Gorky, Dostoevsky, *The Communist Manifesto*, Emile Habibi, Mahmoud Darwish, and Ghassan Kanafani's book on the 1936 Arab rebellion. He has become a publisher for the cause: his first book was devoted to the drawings of Naji el-Ali.[11] He has recently published a guide to resistance behind bars, with one thousand copies printed. His customers are the middle classes, and a growing market of gifts for prisoners. The bookstore was vandalized by soldiers several times at the beginning of the Intifada and during the reoccupation of 2002. His beloved nephew, a student leader, a Communist who dreamed of running a bookstore, was arrested, tortured, and given three life sentences for preparing a suicide attack (a pretext, according to K.).

K. joined the Communist Party at the age of fifteen, explaining: "The occupiers prevented me from going to school; the party is my home; that's where I learned how to live." He is a member of the executive committee of the Party of the People (Communist), responsible for prisoners and culture. The Palestinian Authority?

"It's a historic conquest by the people; it has made many mistakes, but I still support it. It made possible a democracy that does not exist in any other Arab country. My bookstore was never interfered with, whereas I've had books banned from being sold in Jordan in the midst of an international fair. I was summoned one day by the Information Minister, in the presence of Arafat, who said; 'It's not serious if I'm insulted; you can sell the book.'" [He was, however, barred from selling the two books by Edward Said on Oslo.]

Hamas?

"It's a respectable fraction of the resistance. You can't punish the people for making a democratic choice. Hamas filled a vacuum that we allowed to develop. We have differences with them, but we will never be against them."

Car theft is one area of active cooperation between Israelis and Palestinians. You can find an excellent car here for two or three thousand shekels. It will have been stolen in Israel and driven through the checkpoints by an Israeli with its yellow license plates (Palestinian plates are green) and changed hands when it reached Nablus, where it will be driven undisturbed with no registration and no insurance. Many taxis are stolen cars that have been remodeled and painted yellow. Locals can pick them out because the names painted on the doors ("Paradise Taxis," "Magic Taxis") identify companies that do not exist. I have also been led to believe that the weapons Palestinians use also come from traffic between Israeli and Palestinian gangs, but this is not a subject easy to talk about.

A Day in the Country. Burin, south of Nablus, is a beautiful old village, a way station on the road between Jenin and Jerusalem under the Ottoman Empire. The direct road is blocked, so you have to go through the Hawarra checkpoint and then retrace your steps to reach the village: fifteen kilometers instead of three, not counting the time spent at the checkpoint. Graffiti and flags show that Burin is a stronghold of the Popular Front for the Liberation of Palestine (PFLP). The high school was built in 1927, and it has been coeducational ever since, which is not very common. Since it is located in a zone where the occupation forces have forbidden construction, its second floor is built on piles above the old buildings. A dozen teachers invite us in—the children are on vacation—and tell their story.

"The village is surrounded by settlements on all the hills, among them Yitzhar, which, founded in 1983, is one of the most extremist in the West Bank. (Extremism is almost a commonplace. Where are the peaceable settlements? There must be some!) They are Russians and other Eastern Europeans and Falashas [Ethiopian Jews], and they're all hung up because they don't speak Hebrew as well as we do. Every year they set the crops on fire—even on Shabbat. They chop down the olive trees, and in the springtime they steal lambs. In the fall they shoot at people harvesting olives, even at internationals. You can always complain to the Coordination in Nablus, a "complaint against X" that will never go anywhere. Sometimes we make the effort to call the army to tell them that the harvest will take place on such and such a day at such and such a place—they always get there after the settlers have left. The students used to cultivate the land around the village that the school owns, but now it's too dangerous.

"The waste water from the settlements is dumped on our land, so our two springs, which have been famous for centuries, are polluted, which has caused many cases of hepatitis. The water shouldn't be used for washing, and we ought to drink bottled water, but people are so poor. . . .

"Our salaries haven't been paid for three months [since the boycott of the Hamas government began]. A taxi from the Hawarra checkpoint to Burin (six kilometers) costs 10 shekels round trip, which comes to 200 shekels a month. Some of us live in Tell, a village three kilometers from here. The road between here and there is blocked, and we have to go through Nablus! One of us bought a donkey to go over the hills: the soldiers beat him with the stick used to prod the donkey. Most teachers in the school have a second job: they're farmers, or they raise sheep. The physical education teacher, who has twelve children—one of his sons is serving a six-year prison term—drives a taxi.

"We try to soften the children's feeling of injustice, to make them think about other things, but we're caught in a contradiction: we teach them the Declaration of Human Rights, the right of everyone to an education, and they say to us: 'None of that's true! Why can't anybody in the world stop the Israelis?' We have become specialists in transmitting lies. We should be kind and gentle, but we're carrying around a load of worries and frustrations. In the morning, we run a small school radio station, where students tell stories they make up. What are they about now? A martyred father, soldiers coming into the house, a visit to a brother in prison, aggression by the settlers. . . . The older ones tell us: 'You've failed; you're telling us nonsense; we have to invent our own way of resisting, even if people call it terrorism.' That's how it comes about that we teachers are accused of fostering terrorism."

In one room in the school, there are twenty computers, gifts from the diaspora of the village, which has an old tradition of emigration. When asked if schools receive any help from the government, the teachers reply: "We've never seen a representative from the Ministry of Education. They ought to help us, at least symbolically. Never. Everything that's done here, we do by our own efforts."

*   *   *

The maneuver aimed at turning the people
against Hamas is failing, at least in Nablus. The
people I speak to, even those close to Fatah, all
agree that the results of the elections should be re-
spected. The fact that Fatah is the party of collaboration with the occupiers is now more than
obvious to the inhabitants of various political
stripes I meet. The governor of the province of
Nablus, a sort of Fatah administrator with no
power, has forbidden Y. to give the teachers of the
city and surrounding villages funds raised in
France, on the grounds that this would be playing
into Hamas's hands. The money is supposed to go
back to Paris, but it does not.

The head of Radio Najah is twenty-seven years
old. He learned journalism on the job, and he persuaded the university in 2003 to sponsor and support an independent radio station. One of his
most popular programs, aside from the morning
news, is "Open Visit," on which families talk to
prisoners every Thursday.

"How do you go about gathering news?"

"I have networks of friends, contacts in every

neighborhood and every milieu. And people call
us up to say: 'You should talk about this or that.' I
try to verify the rumors that are circulating in the
city. For example, I was told that the aid coming
in was distributed to Hamas members first. I
talked to the local party leadership, and they told
me that it wasn't true, but I was able to show that
this was what was really happening. Last year, we
proved that the Palestinian Authority was distrib-
uting products after their expiration date. We
forced them to burn them, and the leaders responsible were fired. Now there's a campaign to stop
people driving without insurance: people were
waiting in line for more than eight hours. I did
some interviews in the crowd, and two days later
the waiting time was down to fifteen minutes, and
the office manager was fired. We've become a
source for the news services of Arab countries, and
even the Israelis listen to us. I read a lot of Israeli
newspapers."

"Have you had problems?"

"I've never been under any direct political
pressure, but two months ago Authority people
[the Fatah presidency] wrote to the dean of the
university to say that things had gone far enough,
and Hamas has exercised the same kind of pressure. The information minister in the last [Fatah]

government threatened one of our staff members. I insulted him on one of our programs, and he caved. There's no one backing me, but I make believe I'm strong, and politicians are afraid of the truth."

Family Life. S., a girl of nine, and her brother J., ten, are being raised by their grandmother in a house in the old city. Their father was sentenced to twenty-two years in prison in 2001; and their mother, to thirteen years. They were accused of trying to plant a bomb in the Tel Aviv bus station. The children haven't seen their parents for three months; they've been able to visit them only four times during the five years they've been in prison in Israel, in two different cities. They've seen their father only behind glass— with handcuffs and his feet shackled. The grandmother cannot go to see her son or his wife: her visits are forbidden "for security reasons," so the children go alone in the Red Cross bus to Ashkelon. Nor can she visit her second son, who was arrested six months later and sentenced to eighteen years in prison.

Soldiers have come to her house four times and trashed everything, as they frequently do to prisoners' families. The "salaries" usually paid to

families of detainees have not been paid for several
months, since the boycott began. The grandmother
can therefore no longer send money to the prisoners. And "normal" food in prison is inedible;
there are cockroaches in the soup. . . . You have to
pay to eat in Israeli prisons.

Meanwhile, the children's uncle has come into
the house. His son blew himself up in Israel in
2002, and the uncle's dearest wish is to recover his
son's body. Was the son a militant? Not at all, not
even a believer, but when the military destroyed
his house, when he realized he had no roof over
his head, no work, no future, he decided to end his
life.

S. and J. are first in their classes. She wants to
be a teacher, and he, a doctor.

At fifteen, A. is one of the youngest to attend
Darna training programs. We visit him and his
grandmother in their house on the outskirts of
Nablus. His mother was released from prison five
months ago. He has a brother who was sentenced
to twenty years in prison three years ago. He goes
to see him every month in Telmond prison near
Natanya. His father has gone and left no forward-
ing address.

His mother comes in, not wearing a veil; she is quite beautiful with her short hair. When she was arrested, A.'s mother was put in the same prison as her older son, who thought she had come to visit him. She never found out why she was arrested: she was told that she was a "danger to Israeli security." In her prison the male and female Fatah and Hamas activists were in separate wings. I ask her what side she was on: Fatah, but this time she voted for Hamas. She went on a two-month hunger strike in prison: there were four roll calls a day, and if a detainee missed one, all the women were subjected to collective punishment. In retaliation, she was prohibited from seeing her son—and now, as an ex-prisoner, she has no visiting rights. She can contact him only through local radio stations. There is a waiting list of several months for telephone calls.

The older son is in charge of the youth in the prison—there are a number of fourteen- and fifteen-year-old kids. He had been contacted by people in Balata camp for a suicide attack. He refused but said he would try to find someone else, and that's why he was convicted and sentenced. The mother went to see the Balata people, but they refused to help her.

The grandmother asks me what I think of

Abu Mazen. I answer evasively, sensing that she wants to speak. In fact, she explains that she wants there to be new legislative elections. The younger woman doesn't want to hear anything more about political parties. A., for his part, thinks that there is no future and that it's useless to waste your time making plans.

The Z family, in the heart of the old city. The father greets us; he is no longer young and he is worn out. One of his sons has been killed, another is in prison, sentenced to five years for "aid to the resistance." Their eighteen-year-old daughter was arrested last week. Her father has been told that she is in administrative detention for four months, but that she would be released if she pays four thousand shekels. In the courtyard is the youngest, a little boy of about two, who bears the name of his dead brother, Jamal.

The mother enters carrying the groceries. She takes off her veil and her shoes. She can visit her son, but she has not seen her daughter since her arrest, "for security reasons." Is this a family of militants, and is that why it has gone through these ordeals? "The old city is a constant target for the army; there is no need to be political to be a part of the resistance; it's a matter of course."

The Red Cross bus leaves for visits at 3 A.M. with all the relatives of prisoners in the area, often with children of eight or ten on their own. The bus cannot stop during its passage through Israel: neither parents nor children can get off to relieve themselves. In the best case, visits last for an hour, through a glass. The return trip is at night.

As a foreigner, in spite of everything I feel a lightness in the atmosphere of Nablus. There is the difficulty of daily life, fatigue, suffering, and mourning, but it would not be accurate to stop there. This is also a city with no police—which means something—no advertising, no human beings reduced to sleeping in the street and begging to stay alive, a city whose population is not reducible to the sum total of its inhabitants. Just as the pressure applied to a fluid can in certain circumstances changes its physical state, pressure in the pressure cooker of Nablus has transformed the population into *a people*. One day, when the country is at peace, when the ruined soap factories and the miserable dwellings of the old city are transformed into luxury restaurants and charming hotels for the Jewish–Arab bourgeoisie and the tourists, the great-nephews of the "martyrs" whose funeral pictures are now scattered among the election posters will perhaps say that, at bottom, those were the good old days.

NOTES

1. The First Intifada began in 1987 and ended with the signing of the Oslo Accords in August of 1993. The Second Intifada (or the al-Aqsa Intifada) began in September of 2000.

2. Hamas (acronym of Harakat al-Muqawamah al-Islamiyyah, translated as "Islamic Resistance Movement") is a Palestinian anti-occupation organization closely related to the Muslim Brotherhood that, since January 2006, has formed the majority party of the Palestinian National Authority.

3. The UN agency has cared for refugees since 1949.

4. Fatah (a reverse acronym from the Arabic name Harakat al-Tahrir al-Watani al-Filastini, literally translating to "Palestinian National Liberation Movement") is a major secular Palestinian political party and the largest organization in the Palestine Liberation Organization.

5. A Palestinian militant group closely linked to the Fatah political party and one of the most active forces in the al-Aqsa Intifada (the Second Intifada). The group is mainly considered a secular nationalist organization.

6. The West Bank was granted to as-Sayyid Abdullah (King of Jordan from 1949 to 1951) in exchange for the near absence of the Jordanian Army in the 1948 war, except in Jerusalem.

7. From 1949 to 1967, the West Bank was under Jordanian control.

8. bin Talal Hussein (King of Jordan from 1952 to 1999) ascended to the throne after the assassination of his grandfather, King Abdullah.

9. President of the Palestinian National Authority since January 15, 2005, Abu Mazen is also known as Mahmoud Abbas. He is a leading politician in Fatah.

10. Terms used by the supporters of Greater Israel to designate the West Bank.

11. A Palestinian cartoonist assassinated by Mossad in London.

II. QALQILYA

The main street running through the center of Qalqilya ends right at the wall surrounding the city, an artificial end of the world where it is very hot, there is no air, and all sounds are muffled. Greenhouses huddled against the wall indicate that this used to be a place for market gardeners, but it is now run down: a few auto repair shops, a few dilapidated houses. One of the people passing by tells us: "We can't breathe any more." He had two floors built over his garage, but the army ordered him to tear them down, because from the top you could see over the wall, which is ten meters away. The street running next to the wall leads to a tree nursery, whose owner is slumped in a sagging armchair. The wall took up ten of his fifteen dunams (1 dunam = 1000 square meters) of property. He keeps working with what he has left, but he doesn't know why, because he no longer sells anything: plants and trees in pots are pressed up against cement. Before the wall was built, the main north–south road in Israel went past the nursery, and Israelis came from all over the country to buy rose bushes and apple trees.

The wall here follows the Green Line.[1] The north gate, which leads directly into Israel, is deserted at this time of day: the few Palestinian laborers who have identity cards with magnetic strips and have managed to obtain work permits go through at dawn. On the metal fence that is painted yellow and lined with barbed wire, a poster bears the usual notices in Arabic and English ("Get your papers ready, etc."). The last line shows a sense of humor that evokes other barbed wire in other times: "Have a good day."

Qalqilya used to be at the junction of three roads: toward Jordan in the east (through Nablus), toward Haifa in the north, and toward Tel Aviv-Jaffa in the west. Today the wall surrounds the city on all sides, over a distance of thirteen kilometers. The only way out is the road to Nablus in the east. For a long time, to get through this single gate to the outside world, you had to go through a checkpoint: it seems that Sharon himself had it removed when he visited the nearby settlement of Alfe Menashe, one of the largest in the West Bank.

★ ★ ★

According to the *Israel–Sinai* road map published by Freytag and Berndt in 1995—a document that is simultaneously objective and unreal, because while all the cities indicated do exist, the roads connecting them on paper are for the most part impassable—I see that I am less than ten kilometers from the place where my mother was born ninety-nine years ago: Petah-Tikvah, a few shacks in the sand at the time of the Ottoman Empire, is now a suburb of Tel Aviv and the site of one of the principal detention and interrogation centers of Shin Bet, the Israeli internal security service. This is the place where the state of Israel was the narrowest in 1967: barely more than fifteen kilometers between the coast and the West Bank, hence the efforts to widen the bottleneck through annexation.

The wall that hems in Qalqilya is made of sections of cement with turrets and surveillance cameras that have appeared in photographs and films throughout the world. When you move away from the city, another system continues the encirclement. In the center, a paved road allows patrol vehicles to circulate. On either side (sometimes on only one side), a fence that is not electrified—which would not be a serious obstacle because it would only have to be breached at one spot for it to become inoffensive—but electronic: the slightest contact sets off an alarm; the surveillance cameras set at intervals of fifty meters locate and photograph the intruder, and jeeps arrive within a few minutes. The two fences bordering the road are flanked on the outside by a deep and wide ditch and three rows of barbed wire. This complex is bordered on each side by a "buffer zone" that has been cleared by bulldozers, in spots as wide as several hundred meters. This system can be called a "wall," because it is just as impassable as concrete. It has the advantage over concrete, one might say, of being transparent, but it destroys the landscape much more extensively than the track of a high-speed train or the footprint of a highway.

East and south of Qalqilya, this wall follows a complicated path in the shape of inverted loops: one surrounds Qalqilya with an opening to the east, in the direction of the West Bank; the other surrounds the settlement of Alfe Menashe with an opening to the west, in the direction of Israel. This line, which must have given the bureaucrats of the army of occupation a good deal of work, still has a few defects. The road reserved for the Palestinians goes through the village of Beit Amin: the settlement of Elkana is separated from the village only by the width of the wall, and from the buffer zone you can see the settlers as though you were next to them. At another spot, the entire village of Azzoun Atma has been left entirely on the "Israeli" side (in quotation marks because it is well to the east of the Green Line, several kilometers inside what is theoretically Palestine). The village is connected to the West Bank by a special passage through the wall, which is open only in the morning and the evening, when it is open. It is permanently guarded by soldiers, because it also controls the road for the settlers of Sha'arei Tikvah (the gate of hope).

At times, the car goes through a narrow corridor between two walls, with Israel to the west and Alfe Menashe to the east. When we reach the town of Habla at the end of the trip, we are a few hundred meters from Qalqilya. A tunnel, financed by the European Union (EU), enables you to cross this distance by going under two parallel walls and the main east–west road reserved for settlers, connecting Israel to the major settlement bloc of Ariel.

I'm aware that I am describing with difficulty a complex arrangement: in fact, as I've traveled around the region, I have gradually stopped trying to understand the reason for any particular wall, or road, or fence. In reality they have no precise logic. This does not mean that the whole arrangement is irrational: the loops of the wall, the roads reserved for settlers and the occupation troops, the fences surrounding the twenty-five settlements in the region and their fifty-five thousand inhabitants form a network of control over the landscape and transform it into a dismal electronic game. I understood here that *the term wall is deceptive*. Even if you know that its path is anything but straight, the word suggests a linear separation, like the one between the two Germanies or Czechoslovakia and Bavaria before 1989. Here there is nothing of the kind. The wall is an element on which an entire network is based. This two-dimensional—three-dimensional in spots: there are eighteen tunnels like the one in Habla in the West Bank—network is not a way to protect the settlements. It has a different purpose, to snare the Palestinians in its coils, to trap them within enclaves where their lives will not be— already are not—possible. As you travel around the Qalqilya region, you see before your eyes the advanced development of the three phases of the annexation: isolate, enclose, clear out.

The two brothers with whom I'm staying and who are my guides in the region, A. and S., live in Azzoun, a large farming town a few kilometers east of Qalqilya. They run a tiny shop selling and repairing mobile phones on the main street, one of the few with any customers. The fact is that it's almost impossible to live in the West Bank without a mobile phone: you don't make appointments, you say: "When you get through the checkpoint, call me."

A. explains local politics to me. The municipal council has twelve members, all of them from the town's great families—from one to three councilors per family, according to its size. "So it's not a political election?" I ask. "Yes and no," A. answers: on the one hand, it's a clan election, but on the other, the elected council leans toward Fatah.

For R., a civil engineer who works for the municipality, the situation in the village is catastrophic, because farming no longer produces any revenue. The villagers can no longer sell produce outside, and they can't sell in town because no one has any money. The only sources of revenue were salaries of the Palestinian Authority officials and financing of projects by donor countries. Both sources have dried up since the boycott of the government. Among the projects are public buildings, schools, road repairs, and so forth, financed by the United States,[2] the World Bank, and the EU. Each project provides a livelihood for about a hundred people in the village. Projects under way will be completed, but all new ones are blocked.

The village has two water sources but has the right to pump only forty thousand cubic meters per month. The Israelis come regularly to verify that this quantity is not exceeded (the region sits atop the great Western Aquifer, now largely diverted by the occupiers by means of wells dug on the west side of the wall). Electricity is supplied by an Israeli company, but since bills are no longer paid, it may be cut off at any moment. "Do you help the poorest?" I ask. "How do you expect us to help them?" A. answers. "The town doesn't have a penny. We ourselves no longer get paid. People can't pay their taxes, and we no longer get anything from the government. If they keep strangling us, there will be terrorism in Israel."

One of the settlers' practical jokes is to pollute Palestinian land. A settlement such as Elkana, atop a hill, dumps its waste water below, toward Beit Amin, which is pervaded by an indescribable stench. Near one of Azzoun's water sources, on the road to Jayyous, you go past a mountain of garbage as high as a slag heap in the north of France. Settlers come there regularly to empty their garbage

bins. Analyses of the water show that it contains
high levels of toxins, but, as people say, they have
no choice but to drink it.

In the main street of Qalqilya, over which float
the green flags of Hamas, the sidewalks are shel-
tered from the sun by tile awnings supported by
wooden pillars. The street is shared by cars, horses,
donkey carts, and horse carriages driven by children. In the shops, you can find live chickens,
sport shoes, cans of paint, women's negligées,
dried fruit, and couches like those decorating all
the living rooms in Palestine. There are people but
few buyers. The shop owners have taken their
chairs out onto the sidewalk and watch the time
go by. Many shops are closed (40 percent according to a leaflet published by the Office for the
Coordination of Humanitarian Affairs, a United
Nations agency. Probably not so many on the
main street, but it's true that the adjoining streets
are deserted).

On the terrace of the only café open to the outside, a man smoking a water pipe tells me how
beautiful life was before the Second Intifada: people

went off to work in Israel freely; with no permits, you could go everywhere; the market gardeners of Qalqilya supplied the entire West Bank with fruits and vegetables, and Israelis came to shop here. Many signs in Hebrew are left over from that time. Oddly, the dentists' signs are in Cyrillic characters—maybe impoverished Russian immigrants came here to be treated.

A police car followed by two vans filled with armed men in uniform goes up and down the street several times. Are they Fatah security forces showing their muscle in this town that backs Hamas? What happens when a convoy like this encounters Israeli military vehicles, which are present on all the roads? Probably nothing. Collaboration between the army of occupation and the Palestinian security forces in the "antiterrorist fight" was one of the pillars of the defunct Oslo Accords, and perhaps there are traces of it left.

Hamas 3. In Qalqilya. You can enter the Qalqilya town hall freely: no police, no inspection. Not having been announced or introduced, A. and I take only a few minutes to get to the mayor's office, a huge room where old men are reading newspapers, veiled women are typing on computers, and men with various styles of beard are having noisy discussions. The mayor, who is tall, with a short gray beard, and as elegant as an aristocrat in a Buñuel movie, walks in. He was elected while he was in prison.[3] He asks us to excuse him and turns us over to one of the municipal councilors.

"How do people manage to live with the wall and now the boycott of the government?"

"Palestinians adapt to every situation. But it's true that things today are very hard, because we're under a double siege, by the Israelis and by the countries that have cut off aid to the Palestinian people. We feel particularly bitter toward Europe, which is trampling on its own principles."

"Is the municipal council entirely Hamas?"

"The fifteen municipal councilors were elected on the list headed by Hamas. Our program was summed up in a few lines: transparent accounts, teamwork, constant contact with the people. Today the city's accounts are public, they're printed in the newspapers, and anyone can come to consult them here. We take all complaints into consideration; you can see the answers posted in the lobby."

"What are you doing to help people who are no longer being paid because of the boycott?"

"We encourage those who have the means to help the most destitute. We don't put pressure on them; we act as intermediaries: the city government guarantees loans, at the very low rates authorized by

Islam. We have also reactivated the 'fund for the poor' to cover expenses that some people can no longer pay: water, electricity, the fee for garbage removal . . ."

"In your opinion, how will the current crisis between the elected government and the president's office be resolved?"

"We think there will not be a great cataclysm, despite the serious incidents that occasionally occur. We are looking for ways to overcome our differences with the people around the president, but we reject the idea of a referendum [proposed by Abu Mazen on the "prisoners' proposal"]. A consultation of that kind can only take place in a quiet situation. It's absurd to talk about a referendum to people under siege who don't have enough to eat."

[This reminds me of the clever joke made by Ariel Sharon adviser Dov Weisglass, which made the prime minister and the entire Israeli cabinet collapse in laughter in the fall of 2005: "We won't starve the Palestinians; we'll just help put them on a little diet."]

Three Villages. From the roof of the town hall in Jayyous, a hilltop village, you can see a kind of demonstration of the function of the wall. The broad plain that extends in the distance to

Qalqilya, and further on to the sea, is spread out before your eyes like a map. In the foreground is the land that still fully belongs to the village: olive trees, lemon trees, greenhouses. Then comes the electronic wall, running roughly north to south, blocking the landscape as far as the eye can see. Beyond that lies the confiscated land that stretches as far as the red roofs of the settlement of Zfim in the distance. You can see the north gate cut into the wall (the south gate is farther off, hidden by the hills).

The municipal council has nine members, five Hamas and four Fatah. The mayor: "Jayyous used to have thirty-five thousand dunams of land. We lost 2,000 in 1948. The construction of the wall took away 500. And now, behind the wall, there are 9,000 dunams of lemon trees and guava plants, 200 greenhouses, and twenty thousand olive trees. We need a permit to go work on our land: out of one hundred requests, the Israelis may issue five permits. I myself don't have one. A French friend in the Red Cross went to request one for me in the settlement of Kadumim: he was refused. In any case, it's very hard to work: the north gate is open twelve hours a day but never at the same times, and most of the time the soldiers won't let the tractors through. The south gate is open for half an hour three times a day.

"We have no way of selling what we produce. A case of twenty kilos of lemons is sold in the market for 5 shekels (a little more than US $1). Out of that, you have to take 2 shekels for the driver, 2 for labor, and that leaves 1 shekel for the farmer. To sell in Ramallah or Nablus, you have to go through checkpoints and change trucks at each one. When the produce gets there, it's in such bad condition that it can't be sold. And exporting is impossible.

"Water? The village's six wells are on the other side of the wall. We are forced to truck in polluted water from Azzoun.

"In short, most people here have nothing left to live on. And now they're talking about building another settlement on the other side of the wall for the settlers from Gaza. We fought barehanded with the internationals against the bulldozers; they fired tear gas at us, they shot at us, and it did no good: you can see the wall. But it's true that it helps to break the silence."

We head down toward the north gate— barbed wire, two yellow metal fences with hinges, a guard post surrounded by sandbags. The soldiers keep a couple of old peasants coming back from their fields in a donkey cart waiting under the burning sun. F., who is with us, points to a house, the only one on the other side of the wall. The farmer refused the money the army offered him to leave: "Even if you fill my house with gold, I won't leave." On the side where we are, F.'s uncle has a small farm next to the wall, where he raises sheep and goats and grows vegetables. He replanted along the fence about twenty olive trees that were uprooted when it was built. The army has ordered him to clear them off, because the buffer zone is supposed to be 200 meters wide at that spot. No one knows when they will come with bulldozers.

I don't understand clearly these different levels of legalism: why does the army offer money on one side and send in bulldozers on the other? Is it because the farmer who refuses gold is "in Israel," a country where they respect the law?

Further north, on the road to Tulkarem, Ar Ras is another beautiful hilltop village, on the first range of hills after you leave the coastal plain. The green flag of Hamas flies over most houses. A peasant passing by explains that the wall passes through downhill from the village and cuts it off from almost all its land. But the situation is worse than in Jayyous, because the only gate giving access to the fields is three kilometers away, and between the village and the gate, the army has set up a checkpoint, so that farmers have to go through two inspections in a row, the checkpoint and then the gate in the wall. He himself has not been able to get to his fields since the wall was built. No new permits have been issued for months.

On the other side of the wall, you can see the hamlet of Jbarrah, which is totally isolated. Its 250 inhabitants can enter Palestinian territory only through the gate in the wall. Plans exist, says our momentary guide, to push back the wall and put Jbarrah back on the "right" side, but nothing has happened so far.

Mas'ha is a large town in the plain, about fifteen kilometers southeast of Qalqilya. That is where the first camp to resist construction of the wall sprang up in 2003, bringing together villagers, internationals, and Israelis. Now the wall surrounds the village on three sides, and the site of the former camp is included in the buffer zone. In Mas'ha, there isn't even a gate in the wall: to reach the olive groves on the other side, you would have to cover fifteen kilometers. In other words, the village has lost the bulk of its land.

Before the construction of the wall and the expressway connecting the Ariel settlement bloc to Tel Aviv (reserved for Israelis), one of the largest markets in Israel was located on the "old" Tel Aviv road. O., our guide in the town, had three shops there, which he rented for US $3,000 a month. The traffic was so heavy that it was hard to cross the road: on busy days, police had to direct traffic. Today, the wall cuts across this road. On the deserted roadsides, iron sheds stretch out for at least two kilometers, with signs in Hebrew and Russian, vestiges of a glorious past.

The village is gloomy, as though it had been psychologically abandoned by its inhabitants: there are no signs of the fighting spirit a visitor might be able to see—flags, graffiti, community organization headquarters open to the street, happy greetings from children. Maybe merchants are more easily demoralized than peasants. Maybe a village in the plain gives in more easily than a village perched on a hill.

But there is one example of Palestinian ingenuity. The road that connects Mas'ha to Zawia, a neighboring village, goes through a tunnel under the Ariel-Tel Aviv expressway. Just before the tunnel, a dirt path cuts away from the little road and heads to the top of the hill on which the expressway runs. Mornings, especially at the beginning of the week, dozens (I'm told "hundreds," I must admit) of Palestinian workers get into Israeli taxis that stop for a few seconds to pick them up and take them to Tel Aviv. And at the end of the week (today), they return in the opposite direction, on the other side of the expressway. There, as near an "official" checkpoint, taxis wait for customers, stalls sell fruit and cold drinks, itinerant and improvised Palestinian life springs up in the most improbable spot, born from the sorrows of the occupation. It seems that the soldiers are aware of what's happening, but they let it go on. In case there is an alert, for an attack or something else, they set up a mobile checkpoint 100 meters before the tunnel.

On the road out of Azzoun to the west, on the way to Jayyous, a brand new hospital financed by the English is waiting to be equipped. Fifty yards further on is the village's second water source, created and equipped by USAID, with a well 250 meters deep. A group of young people, recruited and paid by an Italian NGO, is working under a hot sun on the retaining wall for the hospital land. They are paid 50 shekels a day. With the boycott of the elected government and the blocking of new projects, this international aid has changed from one day to the next into a means to exert pressure on an entire people.

A rumor is circulating that a wall is going to be built right here, level with the village. The land swallowed by annexation is spreading at great speed.

This afternoon, A., my host, is going to the social center in Azzoun to see a film on the life of Mahatma Gandhi. Most Palestinians I meet think that armed struggle and the militarization of resistance lead nowhere, but as to what a nonviolent resistance might look like, I hear nothing clear, at most vague and slightly nostalgic formulas: "return to the resistance of the First Intifada, create popular resistance committees." And at times I sense that Ghandi has been misunderstood—nonviolence is seen as an end in itself. The new forms of struggle are yet to be invented.

Everything Comes from Israel. Palestine—or at least the West Bank—is the only country where it would be impossible to boycott Israeli products, unless you wanted to return to the Bronze Age. Electricity, gasoline, gas canisters, milk, flour, all essential products come from Israel. To build a house, cement, scrap iron, plaster, and paint come from Israel. And even, which is more surprising, most fruit and some vegetables: peaches and apricots, which are in season, come from the Golan and Galilee. Onions and watermelons are displayed in boxes with Israeli brands—and this is not reused packaging. I am given these reasons: (a) With the wall, our best land for fruit trees and vegetables has been confiscated; (b) Israeli farm products are subsidized and come on the market at lower prices than ours; and (c) Our trucks cannot travel freely, while Israeli trucks go everywhere without inspection. To these certainly accurate explanations, perhaps should be added the traditional character of Palestinian peasants, who have been cultivating their olive trees in the rocky soil of the hills for centuries and have no thought or desire to farm other products or to venture into other occupations.

The limitations on movement and the requirement that all imports and exports go through Israel mean that in Palestine almost nothing is manufactured any more. By stifling all means of livelihood from agriculture and industry, the Israelis are winning on several fronts. The first and most important aim is to weaken the spirit of resistance through poverty and chronic unemployment (66 percent in Qalqilya). On the other hand, even if they are poor, the three million inhabitants of the West Bank represent a far from negligible market. In addition, by keeping the Palestinians' heads under water, the Israelis avoid the potential competition of a neighboring country with a less costly labor force. The dependency in which the Palestinians find themselves on those who can from one day to the next deprive them of fuel and plunge them into darkness should also be mentioned.

Holocaust. The Palestinians whom I met in Nablus generally had some political education, and the idea never entered my mind to ask them whether or not they believed in the existence of the gas chambers. Here it's different. A.'s brother-in-law, an affable man, a construction entrepreneur who went to school in the Gulf, explains to me that the Holocaust is the greatest lie of the twentieth century, and that it's not surprising that Arafat was always a traitor to the Palestinian cause, because . . . he was Jewish.

A., a very lively young man who repairs mobile phones in the shop of the two brothers, learned in school that the Germans killed the Jews. He himself thinks that the Jewish leaders (he says "the aristocrats") had an agreement with the Germans. Why? So that the Jews who were left could go to Palestine.

One of the many nephews in the family is sixteen: his teacher told him that the Holocaust was a lie. Books? No, there was nothing on the subject, because Europe finances their printing. And what does he think? That it's a lie, a propaganda success of the Jewish lobby. He has never heard the name Auschwitz.

According to A., the younger of the two brothers with whom I'm staying, the idea that the Holocaust is a Zionist invention is more than widespread in Palestine. As for himself, he thinks there were massacres, but not as much as they say, not six million, that's impossible.

The negation of the Nazi genocide is based on a kind of twisted syllogism:

- the Jews have stolen our land and are persecuting us,
- the Holocaust is their moral justification,
- therefore the Holocaust does not exist.

In the course of these conversations—and more generally—I've always let it be known at one point or another that I am Jewish, without provoking any surprise. Most Palestinians, including those least informed about what is going on in the outside world, know that there are Jews who support them.

★　★　★

The people I speak to often explain that they have nothing against Jews as Jews. "We've always lived on good terms with them" comes back as a refrain, even among young people for whom the only Jews they know are soldiers and settlers. The negation of the genocide is not part of a European-style, anti-Semitic arsenal: it is the rectification of a historical mystification whose purpose is to justify their own persecution.

But this justification cannot excuse the negation of historical fact. It would be well, in my view, for Arab intellectuals, Darwish and the others, to get to work, to follow the example of Edward Said, to denounce those who are compromising the future of their young people by falsifying history.

The business of the new wall at Azzoun didn't take long. Today (June 7, 2006), an order signed by the military governor is distributed to the population: 894 dunams will be expropriated in Azzoun and Habla for the construction of a road directly connecting the settlements of Maale Shamron and Alfe Menashe to Israel.

NOTES

1. The Green Line is the 1949 armistice line, which served as the border between Israel and the West Bank under Jordanian control until the June 1967 war.

2. The U. S. Agency for International Development (US-AID) is one of the federal agencies most involved in the worldwide counterrevolution.

3. In a few weeks the mayor will be one of the elected officials kidnapped by the army of occupation.

III. HEBRON

The road out of Jerusalem to Hebron goes past an endless series of settlements, Gilo, Gush Etzion—Greater Jerusalem advancing toward the south. Beyond the settlement of Efrat, you are in Palestine, in hills covered with vines (almost trees, horizontal arbors two meters above the ground, like those that can be seen in Italy). Vines accompany the traveler entering Hebron all the way to the center of the city, in vacant lots, on construction sites, in the interstices of the ancient stones.

It is sometimes said that in Hebron 400 settlers protected by the army are making life impossible for 130 thousand Palestinians, a situation that is so extravagant that it has to be seen to be believed. Yet it is not immediately visible to the arriving visitor because the outskirts of the city resemble those of other large urban areas in Palestine—dusty streets, mostly dilapidated buildings, many half-built, some brand new as ugly as those in Ramallah (the latest fashion is for double tile roofs with four slopes, resembling a pagoda).

Things get complicated toward the center. Everything, however, can be summed up in a simple sentence: Hebron is divided into two parts, H1 (eighteen square kilometers, 100 thousand inhabitants), under vague Palestinian control, and H2 (five square kilometers, the heart of the city, thirty thousand inhabitants, plus the 400 settlers), under complete Israeli control. The history of this division was told to me in several ways, but I think I can reconstruct the following process. As for many current disasters in Palestine, everything began with the Oslo Accords of 1993: they provided for three territorial categories: Area A under Palestinian autonomy, Area C completely controlled by the army of occupation, and intermediate Area B, with Palestinian civil control and Israeli security control. According to the agreement on Hebron signed in the aftermath of Oslo, the city was partly in Area A and partly in Area C.

The massacre of twenty-nine Palestinian worshipers in the tomb of the Patriarchs (known here as "the mosque of Abraham") by the settler Doctor Baruch Goldstein during Ramadan in 1994 was a kind of September 11 for Hebron. It was followed by demonstrations throughout Palestine that were very harshly repressed. According to the well-established principle that the victims are the ones who must be punished, Hebron was placed under curfew, total for two months and then covering the old city for six months longer. This was the point at which the physical division of Hebron was established with checkpoints, metal fences, barbed wire, cement blocks in the middle of the streets, a whole system isolating the center of the city and cutting it up into enclaves between which travel—on foot or by mule, because no Palestinian car can enter H2—is possible only by making long detours. Imagine for a moment that in Paris a square running from the Pantheon to the Invalides, the Gare Saint-Lazare, and Châtelet was encircled and blocked off. It was already shocking that the place de la Sorbonne and the rue Saint-Jacques were blocked by metal plates in the spring of 2006. The division of Hebron, made official by the Netanyahu government in 1997, is not indicated by signs as in Berlin in the past: the settlers have removed them because, as far as they're concerned, the entire city belongs to them.

The 400 settlers live in H2, in four main settlements (Avaham Avinu, Beit Romano, Beit Hadassa, and Admot Yishai). These are large buildings or groups of buildings in the old city and on the hill of Tel Rumeida, which borders it on the west. But settlers also occupy the upper floors of many houses in the old city that they have appropriated, particularly above the old market. In the same part of the city, thirty thousand Palestinians are hanging on.

In H1, the "Palestinian" part of Hebron, life might at first sight seem normal, in the particular sense that word has in the West Bank. In fact, many of those who live there are former inhabitants of the old city and Tel Rumeida, who are thus refugees in their own city. And the army is at home here: every night soldiers turn up in one house or another to arrest "suspects"—it's enough to belong to a group or a political party to fit into this category, so that people are careful about what they say, because informers (whom they call "spies") are numerous. The house adjoining the one where I'm staying, in a mainly residential neighborhood of H1, was recently dynamited by the soldiers. A young cousin of the family with whom I'm staying was arrested last week, and no one knows his whereabouts.

This family is tied to the PFLP. The father, who died a few years ago, was a party official who had been jailed and tortured several times. Of the four sons, the two oldest are studying abroad; the third, S., who works in a children's center, is my guide in Hebron; the fourth, T., is studying for the entrance exam to an engineering school. A sister,

R., the youngest, is in high school. The mother speaks English, she has visited her older sons who are in school in Aix-en-Provence and Anchorage, she has no intention of following the custom of looking for wives for her sons, and she votes for the PFLP.

Lives and Fates. S. teaches agriculture at Hebron Polytechnic. He is also an adviser to the Palestinian Authority on environmental questions. He lives northeast of Kiriat Arba (a large settlement adjoining Hebron on the east, populated by religious fundamentalists) in a valley that bears his family's name, S. valley, primarily given over to vineyards.

"In 2000 settlers from Kiriat Arba moved onto a hilltop, on our land. They built houses, surrounded themselves with fences, and started to harass us, attacking children, uprooting trees, and burning cars. We went to the Supreme Court: it decided that they had to leave, but they didn't budge [in Israel, the Supreme Court has two roles: it is charged with determining the constitutionality of the laws, but in addition anyone may file a claim with it against the administration or the state]. One of the settlers' leaders was killed during the Intifada. Thousands of settlers invaded us. They smashed everything in our houses and tried to set them on fire. They hit my father who was over ninety. We called the soldiers, who did nothing. We went to the civil administration [contrary to its name, this is the military administration of the occupation] who sent us to the police, who made us wait for hours, and finally told us they could do nothing.

"Since then, settlers come every Friday to do all kinds of damage on our land, cutting down vines, pulling up posts, uprooting trees. . . . The civil administration asked us to prove that this land belonged to us: we brought out documents dating from the Ottoman Empire. The Supreme Court now has to decide and say if our land belongs to us or if it now belongs to the settlers."

A., a young woman of about thirty, speaks perfect French: she attended the French school in Cairo and got a master's degree in French in Amman. Since she has been living in Hebron for six years—married to a Palestinian, with two children—she has lost her Jordanian citizenship, but she has not become a Palestinian. Most of the many illegal residents here, she explains, are Jordanian. When they are caught, they are sent back to their country. In her case, it would mean prison, because the Jordanians wouldn't want her.

She cannot go through checkpoints, avoids patrols in the streets, and leads the clandestine life of a stateless person. Fortunately, she says, her children have proper papers.

I. invites us into her very poor house on the outskirts of Hebron. She must be about forty-five, perhaps younger. Her face is worn with fatigue, and she chain-smokes. On the wall of what passes for a living room are four portrait photographs in a large frame: the members of her family now in prison. Her husband is one of the PFLP leaders in Hebron. He was jailed for the first time at the age of fifteen and has spent a total of fifteen years in prison. This time, at sixty-five, he was sentenced to seven years, but since he has a heart condition, he has been hospitalized in the prison in Ashkelon, and he may be released, "unless he dies first." She has four sons. Two of them, aged twenty and twenty-one, were arrested three years ago. Soldiers came for them at 4 A.M. They broke down the door and smashed everything in the house. The two young men were later sentenced to five and seven years in prison. They are being held in two different prisons, one in Beersheba in the Negev, the other in Nafha near the Egyptian border. A third son, a twenty-three-year-old university student, was arrested two months ago. He is now being held in administrative detention in the prison of Ofer near Ramallah. The fourth son, aged fourteen, now acts as the head of the household.

The family is a target for the army, like most relatives of prisoners. Soldiers make frequent nocturnal visits, search the house, smash what can be smashed, carry off loot, and leave making threats about the next time.

Every week, I. visits one of her prisoners. Yesterday she made the trip to Ashkelon to see her husband. The Red Cross bus leaves at 4 A.M. and returns at midnight. Since prisoners' "salaries" are no longer paid, she can't send any money to the members of her family, who have no access to the prison canteen or to the telephone. She herself has nothing left to live on, and she borrows from neighbors.

In addition to prison terms, her sons were given very large fines, on the order of 10,000 shekels each. If that sum is not paid, they will not be released at the end of their sentences.

N. owns a shop and a house in the old city, next to one of the main colonies built recently. He is thirty-six, but looks more like fifty. He has been living here since 1997—before that he spent seven years in prison. He has eight children. Before putting up their new building, the settlers offered him a huge sum to leave his house. He refused. They threatened to go after his children. In 1998, when the city was under curfew, his wife was about to give birth, the soldiers kept the ambulance from coming, and the child died. After he again refused to sell his house, the settlers tried to kill his twelve-year-old son by hitting him on the head with rifle butts. They beat his ten-year-old son with iron bars. His wife, who was pregnant again, miscarried in her sixth month after tear gas grenades were fired into the house. He still refuses to sell and leave.

The Old City. F., the best friend of S., my guide in Hebron, lives with his family on the slopes of Tel Rumeida, a kind of hell within hell. He earns his living by reading electric meters for the city government (Fatah for a long time—the last municipal elections did not affect Hebron). I go with him on his rounds, which begin in H1, in the main street market in the city, which is very lively. We stop at a butcher, a barber, and sellers of women's clothes, cassettes, and dishes. Most of them used to have shops in the old city. They were forced to abandon them and unhappily show us the miserable stalls to which they are now restricted. Others—especially vegetable sellers—come from the villages around Hebron. They have to leave home when it's still dark and close very early, because the trip takes hours, and if they stay open past 4 P.M., soldiers come to "search" their shops.

As the street gets closer to the old city, things grow quieter, and at the precise point at which you enter H2, in the old market, only a few people go by, and they walk rapidly. F. continues his work in the few open shops, a stationer, a baker, a butcher. They stay there, he explains, on principle, so as not to give in, but they sell nothing, and they can pay their electricity bills only in installments. Customers do not venture into that desert.

At a level just above the shops, the Palestinians have stretched a large grill across the street, held up by metal pillars. It protects passers-by from the beer bottles, rubbish, and stones the settlers throw from the upper floors of the buildings they have moved into. The splendid stone setting of the old city is concealed behind a whole apparatus of metal and cement, a fabric proliferating like diseased tissue: barriers and fences blocking the streets, steel covering the doors of abandoned shops, little blockhouses protected by sandbags, barbed wire, grills, cement blocks in the middle of the street. All the cross streets are closed off and deserted. But the border between H1 and H2 is not a straight line as the Berlin Wall used to be: it zigzags through the old city to surround one settlement or another and to exclude Palestinian neighborhoods. On roofs and at intersections, surveillance posts are covered in camouflage cloth to make it impossible to tell from the street whether there are soldiers inside. The old city of Nablus felt like a pressure cooker. The old city of Hebron is a ghost town, the setting for a 1970s science fiction movie on the theme of "After the Catastrophe."

R., the youngest child in the family with whom I'm staying, falls ill. Since she has no medical insurance, she cannot be admitted to the municipal hospital—which is probably not a bad thing for her, considering the appearance of the reception area and the corridors. She is sent to the Patient's Friends Society Hospital, a clean and well-kept establishment, where she is properly treated by a doctor who, I gather from a few details, has probably studied in the United States—she is discharged the next day. In this private hospital, run, I am told, by Hamas, a day's stay costs only 500 shekels (about US \$120), but those who cannot pay are not sent away.

Women's Rights. The secretary of the Union of Committees of Palestinian Women receives us in an empty office across from the municipal hospital—she is an alert fifty-year-old, wearing a veil and jeans (almost all women in Hebron are veiled, but the difference is obvious between a religious sign and respect for custom). She works as a volunteer in this association, which has existed in Hebron for twenty years and earns her living as the coordinator of another organization, the Women's Affairs Technical Committee. She is unmarried and has no children.

"How does the occupation affect the condition of women here?"

"The occupation affects everyone. Women have more and more responsibilities: with husbands in prison or out of work, they are forced to go out to work to bring money into the house."

"Do you have the impression that the victory of Hamas in the elections will endanger women's rights?"

"We don't yet have a clear idea of what the Hamas government is going to do. We have no contact, and for now, no problem with them. Before the elections, we spoke at a meeting with Abdelaziz Dueik, the current president of parliament.[1]

He promised us that Hamas would not interfere in our work, and that if the law changed, it would be in a direction favorable to us."

"For example?"

"The prohibition against relations between men and women outside marriage is a central point in Palestinian culture. And women are always the ones who are considered responsible and are punished."

"By whom?"

"By the family. Even today, in the villages a woman may be killed. He promised that if that happened, the law would establish that the brothers or cousins responsible would be tried for murder."

"In your view, what is the most important progress that remains to be made?"

"Raising the age of marriage. Girls are now married off at fifteen or even younger. Families here have six or seven children. It's very easy to marry daughters to the first man who comes along to get rid of them. The minimum age has to be set at eighteen. There is also divorce: a man can divorce very easily, whereas for women it's theoretically possible, but complicated in practice. And take a woman who was married at fifteen, who had children right away, who wasn't able to go to school: when her husband divorces her, she can't work, she doesn't know how to do anything, she's lost. This happens very frequently."

"I see a photograph in your association's newsletter of Ahmed Sadat.[2] Are you close to the PFLP?"

(laughing heartily) "The women in our union are very politicized."

"Do you have—or are you thinking of having—contacts with women's organizations in Israel?"

"We have no contacts in Israel; we have enough to do with women's rights here. Besides, after the business in the Jericho prison [where the Israelis got their hands on PFLP leaders—including Sadat—theoretically under international protection], we no longer trust anyone."

Getting to School in Tel Rumeida. Today (June 12, 2006) is the first day of final exams for high school students in Palestine. By 8 A.M., Ketty is sitting near the checkpoint at the bottom of the hill to make sure that the boys and girls going down to the city are not blocked there, which would put them in danger of losing the school year. She is a large, young American with brown hair tinted blue, a painter from San Francisco. She is part of a small group from International Solidarity Movement (ISM)—mostly from California, living together in a small apartment on the hill. During the school year, their main role is to escort the children to school to protect them from the settlers of Beit Hadassa, who throw stones at them, set their dogs on them, snatch their backpacks, tear off the girls' veils, and knock them down on the steep staircase leading to the school. They themselves (the internationals) are sometimes attacked by the settlers, the majority of whom are American Orthodox Jews (from Brooklyn, according to Ketty). "We do what the Palestinians ask us to do: we help them with children and harvesting olives; we videotape the settlers' brutality; we do our best to help those who have the courage to keep living here."

The street sweeper brings us coffee, the high school students go by carrying their books and greet Ketty by name, and the bored soldiers pace back and forth between the checkpoint and their sentry box protected by sandbags. It almost feels like a village square, except for the rifles.

When the last students have gone through without difficulty, we take a tour around the hill. Once past the checkpoint, you can either go up toward the top, occupied by a military camp and a small settlement, or go straight ahead toward Beit Hadassa. This is a recent complex, all in white, that includes a yeshiva and a large apartment house. Right in front of it, a military post blocks Palestinian access to the street. Opposite the settlement, a steep staircase with uneven steps goes up toward the school: that's where the internationals station themselves every morning during the school year to protect the children on their way to school. The Hebron Rehabilitation Committee recently had a metal handrail installed on the staircase. Toward the top of Tel Rumeida, where a few century-old olive trees are still standing, you can read filthy graffiti on the walls of tumbledown shacks—one is in the form of a command: "Gas the Arabs."

Three Political Positions. A.S.D. is as taciturn and massive as a peasant from the Auvergne. He invites us in cordially, but without the usual outpouring of hospitality.

"My name is A.S.D., and I am a member of the PFLP. I am fifty-eight, I have belonged to the popular front since 1967, and I have been fighting against the occupation ever since then. I went to school in Jordan and Cairo, and I now teach economics at Hebron Polytechnic. I have been prevented from leaving Palestine for twenty years.

"I have spent seventeen years in Israeli prisons, the first time as a student leader in 1972, and the second in 1975 for having tried to set up a joint organization with the Israeli Black Panthers."[3]

"You're a precursor of the joint struggle of Palestinians and Israelis against the occupation?"

"Yes, I worked at the time with Danny Sail,

one of the leaders of the Black Panthers. He was able to escape to France. I never saw him again. I don't know what happened to him; maybe Mossad assassinated him."

"Were they religious?"

"Some were; not all. What brought them together was the struggle against all forms of discrimination, against Sephardim, against Palestinians . . ."

"What is your position in the current conflict between Fatah and Hamas?"

"The PFLP is part of the PLO, which groups together all members of the Palestinian resistance, both here and in the diaspora. We are opposed to Fatah, which has annexed the PLO and emptied it of its content. I won't even mention corruption. We are for a single secular and democratic state in the historical territory of Palestine. To attain this goal, we now lean more toward Hamas than Fatah. We are with them in saying that there is nothing to negotiate for the moment, that the struggle must go on. We have to know how to make alliances, even with people who don't think the way we do about everything: Communists fought with Catholics during the Italian civil war.

"We are against recognition of the state of Israel. But the Israelis have nothing to be afraid of; we have a tradition of living in harmony with the Jews."

"Are you trying to establish ties with Israelis fighting against the occupation?"

"We have a good deal of respect for the real Israeli left. But we can't expect very much right now from the class struggle in Israel. Israeli capitalism is very powerful."

"What do you think of the current attitude of the Arab countries to Palestine?"

(losing his composure) "We consider all Arab governments to be our enemies, perhaps even more than Israel. It's catastrophic that there is no democratic regime, not one, among the Arab countries. We support the revolutionaries in Arab countries. We have to bring down all those corrupt regimes."

"What forms should resistance to the occupation take now?"

"Armed struggle, for the moment at least, can lead only to failure. We have to come back to the form of struggle adopted by the First Intifada, invent a nonviolent resistance, create and lead popular committees. For that, we need a democratic leadership that makes decisions collectively; we have to do away with personal power. A leadership of that kind would be able to talk to the world and coordinate our action with the real Israeli left.

"And besides, we have to change our way of

life, stop depending on Israel for everything, raise chickens, and grow tomatoes in our gardens."

Dr. S. is a gynecologist, a Fatah deputy in the new legislative council, elected on a national list. She was previously secretary of the local branch of Fatah. We visit her at home, where she is joined by her husband, an orthopedic surgeon.

"What steps does Fatah intend to take to renew itself after its failure in the elections?"

"The vote was a punishment for our mistakes. The peace process, which was our work, has led nowhere, and that's what people wanted to sanction. And also corruption, but you should know that those people are now in court." [This is the first time I've heard of any court case, but I don't want to make a fuss.]

"I haven't been here for very long, but I've frequently heard that Fatah refuses to accept the election results."

"Not at all! There are two parties with two different programs; that's all. The Israelis are the ones fomenting conflict."

"Forgive me for insisting, but isn't Fatah trying to exploit the current difficulties to drive Hamas to the wall?"

"Certainly not! The employees whose salaries

haven't been paid for three months are all Fatah people; they're ours!"

"In your opinion, what's going to happen?"

"[Prime Minister of Israel Ehud] Olmert's plan is to crush the Palestinians to drive them to leave. It's an underhanded transfer plan. We have to restore unity to put the economy back on track."

"But a unity government between people who agree about nothing . . ."

(the husband) "You know, the political parties represent at most 30 percent of the Palestinians, and 70 percent are politically neutral. If the peace process gets under way again, they will come back to us."

(she resumes) "The prisoners' proposal is good and it was very widely accepted in the population. Hamas rejected it, but they have nothing but slogans, not a program. They are not realistic. I asked the current Health Minister questions about important issues, chemotherapy, dialysis, transplants. He knows nothing about any of it. They aren't professionals; they're incompetent."

(S., who is with me, in a rather harsh tone) *"But when Fatah was in power, what did it do about all that?"*

"When we started, there was nothing. We

built the whole system from the ground up. Now, Hamas has a much easier job."

Hamas 4. *In Hebron.* M. runs the office of one of the Hamas deputies in Hebron. He is around forty, and he specifies at the outset that he has spent thirteen years in Israeli prisons. He sees us at the appointed time, which is not the norm, making clear at the start that he has only twenty minutes to give to us.

"Many negative things are said about Hamas in France: that you are religious fanatics, that you will transform Palestine into an Islamic republic with sharia law, that you will suppress human rights. How would you answer these criticisms?"

"The current government is the result of democratic elections, under occupation, of course, but conducted according to the rules. Is it reasonable to think that Palestinians have suddenly turned into religious fanatics? Hamas believes that democracy means first of all accepting others, whether religious or not. We think religion is a private matter, a personal question between man and God. We don't require anyone to be religious, to behave like a religious person, On this point and on many others, there is a great difference between Hamas and, for example, the Taliban." [What he says here is in fact in conformity with the doctrine of the Muslim Brotherhood, Warschawski tells me a few days later.]

"It's also said you want to destroy the state of Israel and to deport the Jews to their countries of origin."

"Hamas as a political party has clearly taken a position against violence. Hamas and the elected government are opposed to racism in all its forms. We feel no hatred toward the Jews. They have the right to live here in peace with us as in the past. We are in agreement about the existence of a Palestinian state within the 1967 borders. Let's come back to those borders, and then we'll see. We will not recognize a state of Israel that has annexed half the West Bank and all of Jerusalem. When the Israelis recognize our rights, in words and in action, we will recognize their state."

The treatment of Hamas in the French media is a caricature: the media pretend not to see its development over the last several years that has led it to become the principal political force in the country; no distinction is made between intransigence and extremism. The Hamas leaders whom I met had nothing picturesque about them: they are calm administrators, with reasonable language, with no imprecations, no turbans, no guns. One might say that their speech is tailored for foreign visitors, but since there are hardly any in the cities I went to, this would hardly be a profitable effort.

S. tells me that in his view there are no media in Palestine. Indeed, what has been translated for me shows that *Al-Quds* is on the level of a French provincial tabloid and that "national" television and radio are pitiful. Al Jazeera has a large audience, but it rather resembles, from what I could gather, an Arab CNN. The Internet is a medium for entertainment rather than information. And since people who have the opportunity to travel are few, most Palestinians are not aware of what is happening in their own country. When I tell friends in Hebron what I have seen in Nablus, they listen to me as though I were speaking of a distant city. They are even less informed about what is happening abroad, particularly in Israel: only the most politicized know of the existence of groups such as Ta'ayush ("Life in Common," an organization bringing together Jewish and Palestinian citizens of Israel that organizes convoys of food and medicine to the cities and villages of the occupied territories). Relations with the Palestinians of Israel seemed to me to be very limited. In France during the last war, we listened to London or Swiss radio—here nothing can be expected from the radio and television stations of neighboring countries. Moreover, the difficulties of daily life and the weight of tradition in each region (especially, I was told, in Hebron) mean that the perspective is primarily local. The lack of information is one of the most serious consequences of the occupation, one of the major handicaps for a nonsectarian resistance. Providing a remedy for it would, it seems to me, be more helpful than operating ministries of Tourism, Finance, and Transportation, when there is no tourism, no finance, and no transportation.

More Land, Fewer Arabs. A. H. heads the Hebron office of the Land Defense Committee, an NGO established in 1995 to advise and assist people whose houses are demolished and whose land is confiscated. It has sixteen members on the West Bank, all volunteers.

"When people get a demolition order from the army—usually for having built 'without a permit'—they have one week to file an appeal before a military tribunal in Ramallah (Rejection Military Committee). If the appeal fails, which is what usually happens, they may appeal that decision to the Israeli Supreme Court. We help them through this process. When you say 'without a permit,' you have to remember that no building permits have been issued to the Palestinians for nineteen years, which is a way of limiting the natural growth of the population.

"East of Hebron and Kiriat Arba, the Israelis confiscated a huge territory (more than twelve thousand acres) in 1996, and in 1998 they expelled ninety-eight families that had been living there for a very long time in caves—they were shepherds. They drove them to the south of Hebron in the middle of the winter, in the snow. We helped them and went to the Supreme Court. In 2002, the Court ordered that they be allowed to return to their land. The army now wants to drive them off a second time, even though people have documents going back to the Ottoman Empire showing that the land does indeed belong to them. They are in the process of transforming the area into an artillery firing range, with targets on the hilltops. And a little further south they've established a radioactive waste disposal site.

"North of Kiriat Arba lies another large settlement called Kharsina. There are plans to join them together with a wall, which will isolate some 100 Palestinian families living between the two settlements. Their land will be confiscated, and people will no longer be able to go in or out without a permit.

"The main wall is going to continue by closing off the West Bank on the south and then the east. The entire Jordan valley will remain on the Israeli side. When the Olmert plan is completed, the West Bank will be divided into fifteen territorial units. One the one hand, there will be six groups of Israeli settlements: the Jordan valley; the Ariel bloc, which will absorb the settlements in the Qalqilya-Tulkarem region; the group of settlements north of Jerusalem; Maale Adumim, an extension of Jerusalem to the east, which cuts the West Bank in two; the Gush Etzion bloc, which will also be part of Greater Jerusalem; and the complex formed by the old city of Hebron and the settlements of Kiriat Arba and Kharsina, connected by a single wall. There are plans to build two barrier roads, one between the hill of Tel Rumeida and the mosque of Abraham, the other between the mosque and Kiriat Arba.

"To these six main groups should be added a certain number of isolated settlements, which will be connected to one another: in our region, for example, a barrier road like the ones cutting through the Qalqilya region will connect the small settlements running along an east–west line to the south of Hebron. It will totally isolate the extreme southern end of the West Bank, wedged between the road and the wall separating it from Israel. The way this kind of small settlement is scattered around is not a matter of chance; they are set in places that make control of the territory possible.

"On the other hand, there will be eight Palestinian population centers, with no territorial continuity, connected by a complex of secondary roads and tunnels (there are already eighteen of them in the West Bank, five in the Hebron region), completely controlled by the Israelis by means of walls, gates in the walls, 'terminals,' and checkpoints. You can always call that a 'Palestinian state.' "

There are various levels of credibility in the arguments the Israeli government uses to legitimate the "separation fence." It is obvious that the wall is not being built for security reasons: whoever wants to risk his or her life to get through can (in the West Bank at least. In the Gaza Strip— thirty × ten kilometers—things are different). The fact that the wall's path has been devised to seize the maximum amount of Palestinian land is evident from any map—a proof by absence: the Israelis don't publish any. On the other hand, the role of the wall in giving concrete form to the program of the Israeli "left"—"They in their home and we in ours"—may appear to be a persuasive argument. But it's a complete delusion. One should not think of a "wall," but of a *complex* (wall + settlements + prohibited roads + closed military zones + checkpoints) so that on the other side there can be no "home." Nablus and Hebron are at some distance from the wall, which does not keep them from being completely surrounded and controlled.

A program with the motto "they in their home" would involve dismantling *all* the settlements. "Annexing the settlements closest to Israel" means annexing the bulk of the West Bank and making the rest unlivable. And when you see these impressive blocs of settlements, many of which are veritable cities, the infrastructures surrounding them, and the systematic way in which their locations have been chosen, it is hard to believe that the Israelis would ever voluntarily give them up. The current Israeli government has "given up Greater Israel": for an unrealizable goal it has substituted an objective that bears a different name but comes down to the same thing—with the advantage of being more easily accepted by "international opinion."

The word "wall" is deceptive, as we have seen. The word "occupation" is as well. The word that should be used is "annexation."

* * *

We have news today (June 15, 2006) of S.'s cousin, who was arrested two weeks ago. He is in the prison in Ashkelon, in administrative detention. Administrative detention is handed down for three or six months, indefinitely renewable. It's a form of imprisonment reserved for people against whom there is no precise charge. No indictment, no lawyer, no trial, just prison.

A School Principal in Tel Rumeida. R., principal of the school located on top of the hill, invites us into her house. The windows and balconies facing the settlement of Beit Hadassa are protected by metal grills to protect against stones thrown by the settlers. "It might seem funny," says R., laughing, "it feels like a prison!" The school takes in twenty-five children from six to sixteen years old. The principal has held this position for eleven years and is retiring this year.

"Do you talk to the students about the current situation?"

"They see everything themselves! They're quite aware of what goes on in front of their eyes every day. How can I talk to them about peace and tolerance? They wouldn't believe me."

"What are your main difficulties?"

"Making sure that the children can get to school. The soldiers often stop them at the checkpoint at the bottom of the hill. Then, since we're just opposite Beit Hadassa, settlers throw stones at them, set their dogs on them, grab their backpacks, tear off the girls' veils. . . ."

"Haven't you noticed a slight improvement recently?"

"This morning, settlers came to set the dry grass in my garden on fire. They keep us from mowing it, and when it's quite high, they come and burn it. The fire spread to the olive trees. We called the firefighters, but they took a long time to come because all the roads are blocked. When they finally got here, the water pressure was too low. The soldiers saw everything from the bottom of the hill, but they didn't budge."

"So you're attacked personally?"

"Yes, all the settlers here know me. Three weeks ago soldiers came at night; they made us go outside and searched the entire house, all our things; they turned on the computers and looked at what was in them. I had the impression that they were looking for photographs."

"Has anyone from the Authority ever visited you during these eleven years?"

"Never."

"Are you glad you're retiring?"

"No. This school is different from all the others. It needs someone strong to protect the children, and I'm worried about the future."

Holocaust, Continued. T., S.'s younger brother (twenty-two, in engineering school), doesn't remember hearing about the Holocaust at school. He thinks the genocide did take place but that it's not his concern; it has nothing to do with him. I answer him that Edward Said and Azmi Bishara (a well-known Palestinian deputy in the Israeli Parliment, the Knesset) have a different opinion. That in their view, Palestinians—and all Arabs—have to be persuaded that the genocide played a decisive role in the creation of the Jewish state. The argument (from authority, to be sure, but how can I do better?) clearly makes him think.

Last night (June 16, 2006), S., who has acute hearing, heard soldiers. From the roof of the house we could clearly see jeeps, flashing lights, floodlights, a whole silent uproar a few hundred yards away. S. doesn't know whom the soldiers had come to arrest.

At-Tuwani. Anyone using an ordinary road map to travel around the West Bank would leave himself

open to difficulties. On that kind of map
(Israel–Sinai at 1/400,000), the village of At-
Tuwani is about ten kilometers southeast of Hebron. "Normally," one would head south on the
main road leading to Israel—toward Beersheba in
the Negev—then, turning east, one would reach
At-Tuwani; the whole trip taking less than a half
hour. But difficulties arise as soon as we leave:
since the main road is blocked on the way out of
Hebron, we have to head directly west to the town
of Dura, then turn back east to the large town of
Yatta. This long S-shaped detour on potholed
roads enables us to admire the Al Fawwar refugee
camp, a frightful cast iron and cement slum over
which flies the black flag of Islamic Jihad.

We have to leave our car in Yatta and take a
taxi, because to continue south toward the Israeli
border, we need a special permit, which we do not
have. Bit by bit, the road turns into a dirt track on
which the taxi has to go around or over huge
bumps, the remains of barriers set up by the army.

After a half hour of jolting, we come upon a
military road cutting across the landscape and
blocking us from the hill of At-Tuwani. Soldiers
in a patrolling jeep have seen us coming: they
leave their paved road and head toward us on the
dirt track. Under the burning sun, they take their
time searching the taxi from top to bottom and

verifying my companions' papers (they tell me if I weren't there, the soldiers would probably take pleasure in making them waste the day, or worse). Finally, the taxi is allowed to return to Yatta, and we cross the military road on foot, going through a gap in the eighty centimeter-high wall flanking it as far as the eye can see. Before starting up the path to the hill, we see an astonishing sight: a settler wearing a t-shirt and shorts is jogging along the side of the road followed by an army jeep for his protection.

At-Tuwani is a village with 150 inhabitants that is very old (one thousand years, we are told). The houses are beautiful, which is rare in this region: cubes made of large stones with slightly curved roofs, resembling the flattened domes seen on top of Turkish baths. Some of them are half-caves set into the slopes of the hill.

In one of these houses lives a small group of young women from a North American NGO, Christian Peacemaker Teams (CPT)—three Americans and a Canadian who tell us about the hardships of the village. It is not connected to the power grid. It has its own generator that operates four hours a day. Since it has hardly rained this year, the water source is dry and water has to be trucked in. The nearest hospital is in Yatta, but when the road is blocked by the army, they can only get there by going across the fields by mule or on a tractor. So the village has built a dispensary where a doctor from CARE provides treatment once a week. But the building was put up without a permit (which is never given in any case), and the army has threatened to tear it down several times.

All these misfortunes would be nothing were it not for the close proximity of Israeli settlers. You can see on a hill less than one kilometer away the red-tiled roofs of the settlement of Havot Ma'on. The settlers who have spread here from the old city of Hebron are among the most aggressive. They attack children on their way to school and shepherds guarding their sheep. They poison animals, set fire to the crops or confiscate them, throw dead animals into the wells, attack houses, destroy tractors. The women of the CPT are often attacked when they escort children to school and accompany shepherds in the fields.

A group of deputies in the Knesset, the committee for the defense of children's rights, was disturbed to learn that settlers had attacked school-children coming from the neighboring village of Tuba. As a result, soldiers have been ordered to escort the children themselves, which they do more or less seriously—they have to be watched. In fact, settlers have several times gone after soldiers escorting children.

Recently, there have been three demonstrations in the village. H., the chief organizer, speaks excellent English:

"We're wedged between the settlements and the forbidden road. The bulk of our land is on the other side of the road, and you've seen that it's flanked by a cement wall high enough to block the passage of tractors, carts, and sheep. This wall is forty kilometers long, and over that distance there are only four or five gates like the one you went through to come here. Most farmers are therefore forced to make a huge detour to get to their land.

"The demonstrations, which were nonviolent, were organized on the initiative of the people of this village and the neighboring villages, the first one last April. We asked the people of Ta'ayush, whom we've known for a long time, to join us, because our aim was to draw attention to our unlivable situation, to bring in the Israeli and Palestinian media. The army acted very harshly in repressing the April demonstration. I was arrested and jailed in Kiriat Arba for two weeks. But we started up again in May and again last week, and since there were more and more people, the army didn't dare to act so brutally.

"We think it is important to draw attention to this region, which is doubly occupied, by the settlers and by the army. The settlers have seized our land, and the soldiers protect them. Life here is hell; it is a catastrophe area."

Al Salamyeh. S. was eager to show me this neighborhood on the outskirts of Hebron before I left because "no one goes there, not even people from the city." This suburb on the eastern end of Hebron is in direct and immediate contact with the settlement of Kiriat Arba. To reach it, we have to take a long trip by car, going around the prohibited center of the city. When we get there, the road is blocked, and we continue on foot. On the right, behind a high, electrified fence with surveillance cameras and floodlights, lie the rows of white houses of the settlement. Straight ahead, Palestinians are barred from the blocked road, even on foot. To the left, a narrow, dirt path for their use overlooks what must have been olive groves, now devastated, covered with rubble and charred tree trunks.

On the other side of the settlement, several hundred worshipers, men, women, and children, sitting in the grass, form a large light blue and white circle. While they chant and pray (it is Friday night), they are protected by soldiers—one every twenty yards on the forbidden road—and by civilians armed with assault rifles surrounding the circle. As we go on—the dirt path has faded, and we're now walking through tall grass—we can see on the hill one hundred yards ahead young men throwing stones at two women dressed in black who are scurrying along. Soldiers leave the road and come down into the field to check our papers: in a place like this, a group like ours is obviously suspect. I tell them I admire what they're doing in the country; they don't understand but allow us to go on to Al Salamyeh.

This neighborhood, where more than two thousand people live, has been largely demolished, and *all* the streets are blocked, both those permitting entry and exit and the internal streets (the cement block industry is probably one of the most prosperous in Palestine). To move around the neighborhood or to go anywhere else, the inhabitants can either go on foot or find a donkey. People whose doors open onto the forbidden road have to climb up ladders over their back walls to get home. The shops are closed, the streets are deserted, and people stay in their houses—they've had some practice, because the neighborhood was under curfew for three years at the beginning of the Intifada, and it is reinstated at the slightest incident: it was last under curfew two months ago.

As we walk west toward the center of Hebron, the streets are still blocked, but their appearance is

different. Cinder block gradually gives way to ancient stone. Some streets have even been restored,
as in the Marais in Paris, probably by some international cultural organization, which adds a touch
of strangeness to the desolation of the place. We
finally come upon an Ottoman arch, closed off by
a high steel gate: on the other side, I am told, is the
mosque of Abraham (the tomb of the Patriarchs),
the heart of the city, twenty meters away and completely inaccessible.

We return at nightfall through the fields, but
on a different path—the one we came on is, it
seems, dangerous at this time of night. We have no
difficulty making our way through the stones and
grass: the terrain is fully illuminated by the floodlights of Kiriat Arba.

Saturday Night in Tel Rumeida. Saturday night, it
seems, is the settlers' favorite time to cause trouble
in Tel Rumeida, throwing stones, frightening children, and attacking internationals. Today (June 17,
2006), the evening is quiet. At the main intersection halfway up the hill, three helmeted soldiers
pace around their guard post, encumbered by their
bulletproof vests, their rifles, and their long radio
antennas. A tall American from the ISM, who
usually runs a tea shop in San Francisco, is jug-
gling like a professional with plastic clubs in the

middle of the street to amuse about twenty children who are hanging around. Old people on mules are heading up toward the top of the hill. Settlers come down in small groups—boys and girls dressed up for a party, probably going to dinner in a settlement in the city. They walk faster when they get to the intersection and go straight ahead, not looking at anyone, going through the group of children and internationals as though the street were empty. A man of about thirty—wearing a white shirt and a kippa—paces back and forth with an M16 slung over his shoulder. The kids are now playing soccer with a deflated tennis ball—they say to me: Zidane, Zidane [the former French soccer player of Algerian descent]—they, too, acting as if the soldiers two yards away didn't exist. Night falls, settlers are no longer visible, watchfulness can relax. In the courtyard of F.'s house, Ketty the magnificent and Jonas the tea seller are dancing by torchlight. Children who have come from all around sit in clusters on the walls, chant their names, and give them an ovation.

Breaking the Silence. It is easy to understand how a sect, or a battalion of the foreign legion, comes together and keeps going. More mysterious is the formation of groups of extremist settlers like those in the old city of Hebron or Kiriat Arba.

How do they come together? How can such ho-
mogeneity of violent hatred be created and main-
tained? In Jerusalem, on the way back, I pose the
question to Yehuda Saul. He is a young man of
twenty-four who did his military service from
2001 to 2004. He spent the last fourteen months
in a combat unit in Hebron, manning a kind of
automatic grenade launcher that could fire series
of grenades a great distance.

"I was born in Jerusalem in a right-wing
American Orthodox Jewish family. I went to a
yeshiva. During my military service, I obeyed orders, I fired grenades at apartment houses, I even felt
some pleasure in firing accurately. I had no qualms
of conscience, and I ended up as a sergeant. It was
when I was demobilized that I had an enlighten-
ment: I couldn't continue living as I had, I had to
tell what I had seen, what I had done. I spoke to
comrades who shared that feeling. So, in June 2004,
we mounted an exhibition of photographs, our
photographs: *Bring Hebron to Tel Aviv*. We made the
front pages of newspapers, we were on television,
we had thousands of visitors. The military police
even came and confiscated a few photographs.
Then we established Breaking the Silence, an organization that lets soldiers speak. We publish their
testimony in booklets, on videos, on CDs, on our
Web site (www.breakingthesilence.org.il). We give

lectures in Israel and in Europe; we organize a guided tour of Hebron every week. I devote all my time to it."

"Where do these settlers come from? How can they live with such hatred?"

"In Hebron, most of them are Orthodox Jews of American origin, on the extreme right, as some are in the United States. They are persuaded that the Palestinians—the Arabs in general—are their mortal enemies: they feel not only hatred, but also fear. They constantly rehearse the history of the great massacre of Jews in Hebron in 1929; they are convinced that the event will be repeated at the first opportunity."

"What about the children?"

"The settlers educate their children against the Palestinians. In their yeshivas, they're taught that it's right to do them harm."

"How is it that the army never intervenes?"

"Sometimes there are individual gestures by outraged soldiers, especially at the beginning of their time in Hebron. But in the army you obey orders; you don't take initiatives. And the orders are to protect the settlers, not the Palestinians. Theoretically, that is the role of the civilian police. But those people never do anything because they're afraid of the settlers, afraid of getting hit by eggs or stones, afraid of getting their heads broken."

After they're demobilized, thousand, tens of thousands of young people, says Yehuda, leave the country for a year. Most of them go to South Asia, especially India. Yehuda claims that special institutions have had to be established for those who come back seriously addicted or completely insane.

NOTES

1. Dueik was kidnapped by the Israelis on August 7, 2006.

2. Sadat was secretary general of the PFLP, in jail in Israel.

3. A movement that fought for the rights of Sephardic Jews in Israel.

AFTERWORD

During this month spent in the West Bank, every day was amazing, but my greatest surprise was to see that the idea of a single state in the territory of historical Palestine is now all but obvious. Of the dozens of people from different milieus with whom I spoke, most have said farewell to a Palestinian state or, to put it another way, they no longer want to hear about shams—negotiating tables, peace processes, redeployment schedules, phases I, II, and III. The state they will finally be offered one day, they know, will be designed by an army of occupation, and they are fully aware of all that army's abilities in the realm of false appearances.

On the other hand, the prospect of living in the same country as the Israelis does not seem to them to be at all extraordinary. "We can very well live with the Jews; we've always done it": I often heard these words, even from people who had suffered personally from the occupation. The youngest, the least politically informed, are capable of distinguishing between settlers, soldiers, and the Israeli people as a whole—whom they cannot help but admire, in spite of everything. One evening, I was looking with F., the man who reads electric meters, from the top of Tel Rumeida at the lights of the settlements and the connecting roads. At one point he spoke of the "Jews," but he quickly corrected himself: "I know I shouldn't say that, I should say Israelis, but with those people . . . [the settlers]"

One might object that the people I spoke with are not a representative sample, that assertions about the psychology of peoples are always questionable, that I heard what I wanted to hear, and that in any event the single state is an unrealizable dream, a *utopia*—with all the negative connotations now attached to that word. Perhaps. But we may nevertheless hope that what happened in Lebanon and Gaza in the summer of 2006 will not compromise this improbable opportunity: it is not hatred that predominates in Palestine, but rather an immense and almost naïve *amazement*—what have we done to be treated like this, how can such injustice have lasted for so long, why does the entire world refuse to help us?

EPILOGUE

The state of Israel has now controlled the West Bank and (from outside the electronic fence encircling it) the Gaza Strip for forty years. Almost two complete generations of Palestinians have already been born under Israeli occupation.

But the word occupation is problematic, because it is usually reserved for relatively short and provisional situations, as provided in the Fourth Geneva Convention. Is it still possible to use the word provisional after four decades? For more than twenty years, the Israeli analyst Meron Benvenisti has taken a contrary view and spoken of "irreversibility," that is, of the impossibility of resolving the Israeli–Palestinian conflict by means of territorial partition. I will come back to Benvenisti's arguments and to the question of irreversibility.

In any event, Israeli control of the West Bank and the Gaza Strip is a comprehensive system that the concept of occupation fails to describe completely, and this is what Eric Hazan very aptly and perceptively shows in his reporting from the West Bank. In *Notes on the Occupation* he speaks of "a great bureaucratic-military machine designated by the rather abstract and even deceptive term 'occupation.'"

Some commentators have adopted the term "apartheid" to describe Israeli control over the occupied Palestinian territories and their population. This may be apt provided we do not attempt to apply too literally to these territories what happened under apartheid in South Africa until the victory of the African National Congress. The word "apartheid" in fact means separation, and the apartheid system is a separation unilaterally imposed by a political regime on indigenous populations. Understood in this way, Zionism as a whole is a philosophy and a practice of apartheid. Zionist ideology in fact is based on the hypothesis that a normal society is a homogeneous society and that the ideal state is a mono-ethnic state; it even considers racism (and hence anti-Semitism as well) as a natural phenomenon, namely, the rejection by an ethnic, national, or religious majority of minorities living among it. Hence Jews must remove themselves from the national communities in which they are living and create their own state, as ethnically

Jewish as possible. The "ethnic self-cleansing" that Zionism advocates for the Jews of the world, the 1948 war of ethnic cleansing, the system of segregation applied to the Palestinian minority in Israel—in extreme fashion until 1965, more subtly thereafter—all reflect the same philosophy, which makes separation a value and not merely a political technique that might be useful in certain situations.

After the 1967 war, the system of apartheid underwent new developments. By deciding to colonize the recently occupied territories, various Labor and right-wing Israeli governments created a system of segregation that was both spatial and legal. While legal segregation—settlers living under Israeli law, the indigenous population under a system of military occupation—is inherent in colonization and was established from the outset, spatial segregation did not appear clearly until two decades later. Little by little, the Palestinians were encircled by settlements and roads called bypasses, until they found themselves by the late 1980s in veritable reservations, which the PLO, in the form of a "Palestinian Authority" put in place by the Oslo Accords, was called on to administrate. Here, too, the comparison with the South African system of apartheid is obvious: the "Palestinian zones" have become Bantustans, granted administrative authority, with a president, a flag, and police forces.

In the course of his reporting in the West
Bank, Hazan has very perceptively grasped this
spatial segregation and the insularity imposed on
the Palestinians by the system of occupation-
colonization, a system that has both fragmented
space and shattered indigenous society. Occupation like that implemented by the Israelis in the
Palestinian territories is a veritable nuclear bomb
that has atomized both the social fabric and the
land. Hence the question the writer-reporter asks
himself: is a solution based on the partition between two states still possible? Or, conversely, does
realism—and not diehard extremism—require
that we envision a solution to this century-old
conflict within the framework of a shared state,
whether democratic as in South Africa, binational
as in Belgium, or federal as in Czechoslovakia?
Hazan does not answer this question, thinking
correctly that it is up to the peoples concerned,
and them alone, to find the most appropriate answer, but he points out: "My greatest surprise was
to see that the idea of a single state in the historical territory of Palestine is now all but obvious."

Notes on the Occupation describes not only the system of occupation-colonization, its arbitrariness,
and its brutality. It also paints a picture of the

occupied population. And they are not only victims of the arbitrariness and violence of soldiers,
settlers, and the colonial administration, they are
also resistance fighters. And these Palestinian resistance fighters are represented not only by A.S.D., a
Popular Front militant in Hebron who has spent
seventeen years in prison, but also by R., a school
principal, and I., the wife and mother of political
prisoners. All these men and women resist by refusing to bow their heads and by refusing to accept humiliating offers on the grounds of realism,
preferring to live under the boots of the occupation rather than sign a surrender.

Their refusal was the primary reason for the
victory of Hamas in the last election held in January 2006. Neither a "fundamentalist" vote, nor
even a vote against a peace based on a more or less
honorable compromise, but an expression of opposition to any form of compromise presented in
the guise of "negotiation." When Hazan inter-
viewed the assistant to the mayor of Qalqilya, a
member of Hamas, he did so without indulgence,
but also without the condescending approach that
Westerners have so often when they are con-
fronted with phenomena that escape the beaten
paths of their prejudices. Hazan wants to understand and make his readers understand not only
the reasons for the landslide victory of the Islamist

organization, but also the nature of that group, much more complex and multidimensional than the media, even those with the best intentions, would have us believe.

But what most gives value to this brief report is that it makes us share a perpetual *amazement*—surprising, at first sight, coming from a man who, as doctor, writer, and activist, has over the last four decades seen many sites of conflict, often as a participant, and should therefore no longer be amazed by anything. But the fact is that in the land of Palestine, traditional guidelines for interpreting conflicts, including colonial conflicts, do not work. The question then is to discover the particularities of what Hazan refuses to call the "Israeli–Palestinian conflict," with all that concept implies of false symmetry between the participants. As a surgeon who is able to treat even what is invisible to the naked eye, the author discovers, beyond the underlying causes, nastiness, stupidity, internal contradictions, and lack of coherence—everything else that constitutes the Israeli occupation—and which, if they are not clearly presented, obscure our understanding of the colonial relationship in the occupied Palestinian territories. Because he does not attempt to conceal his amazement, Hazan may help us to go well beyond preconceived images and simplistic ideas.

And it is because he is himself willing to be amazed that Hazan is one of the few political visitors to the occupied territories to be able to write, at the end of his report, the following words: "It is not hatred that is dominant in Palestine, but rather an enormous and almost naïve *amazement*." His own amazement enabled him to grasp the amazement of the Palestinians. Or perhaps it was the discovery of the perpetual amazement of the Palestinians in the face of the injustice whose victims they have been for more than a century, and of the complicit and hypocritical silence of what is known as the international community, that enabled him to see Palestine with the falsely naïve vision of a man amazed.

—Michel Warschawski
March 2007